House Beautiful

The Fabric Style Book

747.9 D38 2007
Dellatore, Carl J.
The fabric style book

MID-CONTINENT PUBLIC LIBRARY
Excelsior Springs Branch
1460 Kearney Road
Excelsior Springs,
  MO 64024

ES

WITHDRAWN
FROM THE RECORDS OF THE
MID-CONTINENT PUBLIC LIBRARY

House Beautiful

The Fabric Style Book

Decorating with Stripes, Plaids, Florals, and More

TIPS AND INSIDER ADVICE FROM
THE POPULAR "SWATCH WATCH" COLUMN

Carl J. Dellatore with Roslyn Sulcas

HEARST BOOKS
A Division of Sterling Publishing Co., Inc.
New York

Copyright © 2004 by Hearst Communications, Inc.

All rights reserved. The written instructions and photographs in this volume are intended for the personal use of the reader and may be reproduced for that purpose only. Any other use, especially commercial use, is forbidden under law without the written permission of the copyright holder.

The Library of Congress has cataloged the hardcover edition as follows:
Dellatore, Carl J.
    House beautiful : the fabric style book : decorating with stripes, plaids, florals, and more / Carl J. Dellatore with Roslyn Sulcas.
    p.cm.
    "Tips and insider advice from the popular Swatch watch column."
    Includes index.
    ISBN 1-58816-268-0
1. Textile fabrics in interior decoration. I. Sulcas, Roslyn. 2. House beautiful. 3. Title.
    NK2115.5.F3D443 2004
    747'.9—dc22
                                    2004003634

10 9 8 7 6 5 4 3 2 1

First Paperback Edition 2007
Published by Hearst Books
A Division of Sterling Publishing Co., Inc.
387 Park Avenue South, New York, NY 10016

House Beautiful and Hearst Books are trademarks of Hearst Communications, Inc.
www.housebeautiful.com

For information about custom editions, special sales, premium and corporate purchases, please contact Sterling Special Sales Department at 800-805-5489 or specialsales@sterlingpub.com.

Distributed in Canada by Sterling Publishing
c/o Canadian Manda Group, 165 Dufferin Street
Toronto, Ontario, Canada M6K 3H6

Distributed in Australia by Capricorn Link (Australia) Pty. Ltd.
P.O. Box 704, Windsor, NSW 2756 Australia

Manufactured in China.

Sterling ISBN 13: 978-1-58816-656-2
         ISBN 10: 1-58816-656-2

Book Design: Alexandra Maldonado

A Note to the Reader: Throughout this book we have used the name of the fabric and the designer to identify each upholstery example. We did this for identification purposes only; for example, as a means of differentiating one floral textile from the next and not as an endorsement of a particular designer or fabric. Because textiles are taken out of production with such frequency and often remain on the market only a very short time, we do not intend this collection of styles as a catalog source. Certainly, if you are interested in a particular fabric you should feel free to contact the designer.

Page 2: *Sometimes, the best way to make a monochromatic statement is to add a new color. This canary-yellow wing chair is notable for a wreathlike design that appears only on the front, but with enough red to tie in with the room. Nailheads become strong visual details on the chair and upholstered ottoman.*

Right: *In a room filled with many shapes, forms, and treatments, the rectilinear windowpane pattern on the curtains works to bring a cohesive sense of order. Narrow valances, trimmed in thick black, accentuate the height and scale of the room.*

MID-CONTINENT PUBLIC LIBRARY - BTM

3 0003 00594126 3

MID-CONTINENT PUBLIC LIBRARY
Excelsior Springs Branch
1460 Kearney Road
Excelsior Springs,
MO 64024

ES

contents

foreword

Each year *House Beautiful* holds events all across the country and around the globe celebrating the world of design. One of the greatest benefits of these events is that we get the opportunity to speak with our readers about the magazine—what they like, what they don't like, and what they'd like to see more of. In the past few years we've seen a consistent desire for more how-to features to help readers bring a look home. After all, appreciating a window treatment or a perfectly appointed chaise in a picture is one thing; transferring it to your own living room is quite another.

By demonstrating how fabric selection can set the tone for an entire space, "Swatch Watch"— one of our most popular columns and the inspiration for this book—provides just this kind of helpful information. Fans of "Swatch Watch" (as well as anyone overwhelmed by the seemingly endless options available to them) are sure to find *The Fabric Style Book* an invaluable resource. May it assist you in creating beautiful interiors throughout your home.

Cheers,
The Editors of *House Beautiful*

Bold stripes are perfectly matched as they run along the back to the seat and down the plinth. Red stripes are positioned exactly on center along the arms. A simple, streamlined look is created by the stripes; no decorative details were needed.

Gardens are busy places, filled with patterns
and textures that compete, yet harmonize.
In this plush living area, stripes and florals in
the same hue of green work well together,
complemented by the solid green daybed.
Sheer curtains keep the room bright while
providing privacy.

preface

Growing up third generation Italian-Irish in Allentown, Pennsylvania, wasn't always a cake-walk for an insatiably creative boy. Luckily, my two grandmothers were on hand to direct my energies. Grammy Rossie, who owned a restaurant and taught me the secrets of making risotto and braising osso buco with two pieces of orange peel, imbued me with her love of cooking. Grandma Rose, an expert seamstress, taught me seam allowances, bias cuts, and the importance of stitch length.

It would be inaccurate to say that my mother always shared my grandmothers' enthusiasm for my ingenuity, but her unwavering strength as the single mother of three children, her steadfast belief in God and morals, and her drive to hold her family together through extremely difficult days shaped the man I would become. Born on May 21, the cusp of Taurus/Gemini, I must have been a handful—a bullish pair of twins to the core. I can never fully express my gratitude to these three women. This book is for my mom, Anne: You are my friend and confidant, and I love you for that.

I hope that the design adage "form follows function" will never be forgotten. Answering the questions of how, why, when, and what (or what if) is, I believe, the basis for all design decisions. Aesthetics play a role, of course, but ultimately your textile selections should take into account such issues as climate, exposure to sunlight, privacy, durability, and accessibility. Choosing damask for the pet- and kid-friendly living-room sofa, for example, makes as little sense as hanging silk curtains in a sun-drenched window. A better choice for the sofa would be an easy-to-clean cotton blend with a vivid pattern to hide dirt and, for the curtains, "faux" silk, fashioned of technologically engineered poly blends, which are often impossible to discern from the real thing.

For those who can afford them, design professionals are important and can ease some of the decisions about which fabrics to use. But it is my hope that the specifics presented in this book might help everyone gain some basic knowledge of how to use fabric in the home in ways best suited for the space. In a world where we find ourselves stressed and overworked, "sanctuary" in the home becomes more and more important. Creating a sanctuary is easy when you understand the basics.

I would like to thank everyone at *House Beautiful* for their help and support. Marian McEvoy, for the basic idea for this book and the freedom to make it fly; Carolyn Sollis and Elaine Wrightman for brilliant collaborations; and Mark Mayfield, for holding firm to this project and bringing it home to the bookstores.

—Carl Dellatore

introduction

The use of fabric in the home is a universal element of interior design. From the oldest form of flax cloth fashioned on a simple loom to the sophisticated brocades inwoven with precious metals in European capitals, fabric has for centuries provided the basis for our needs at home. And whether it be for a country manor house or the steel and concrete architectural wonders of the last decades, almost every design aesthetic employs its own range of fabrics that forms the basis of seating, window treatments, and other details throughout the home.

An enormous number of options are available for the consumer today. Manufacturing techniques have evolved to produce endless varieties of fabric, both inexpensive and costly. The beautiful damask weaves of centuries past have reappeared in updated and fresh versions by means of simple printing processes, making an ambience once exclusive to royalty now available to everyone. With the judicious use of this broad variety of materials, almost anyone can create a welcoming and unique living environment.

While one ought to consider simple rules of thumb (which we will discuss more later), the days of standard design ideas are long gone. Nowadays, burlap may be paired with linen gauze to create diaphanous curtains, which have been freed by modern central heating from the need to safeguard the warmth of the home, as curtains had to do in centuries past. Embossed leather might cover a modern sofa, a great departure from the gauffrage velvet of the French eighteenth-century chalet. Today's home is also a laboratory for an ever-changing world, as can be seen in design showrooms, where fabrics made of rubber, grass, fiberglass, and copper thread are displayed next to chintz, linen, toiles, and damasks.

Today, interior design can successfully link the past to the present for an idiosyncratic and eclectic look; create something completely new; or pay homage to the past. The constant in each aesthetic is the use of fabric, in one form or another. This book endeavors to illustrate some of the ways fabric can create a home that reflects each individual's tastes; to offer explanations of the dos and don'ts of upholstery; and to inspire the creative process.

Fabrics provide color, texture, and mood in a room, evidenced here by pleated lavender curtains with a novel triangular cut-out valance tipped with gold tassels, effects that harken to a Moroccan tent. The whimsically shaped wing chair is fitted with a slipcover whose welting highlights the shape of the chair and matches the curtains.

sofas

Think of the living room and the
first image that comes to mind is
the sofa. It is the one piece of furniture
that sets the agenda for the rest of the
room; the colors, textures, overall scale,
arrangement, and style of decor. And the
sofa's pattern and position in the room provide clues to how the room will be used by
family and guests.

*A garden of giant flowers blooms indoors. The wool rug is hand-needlepointed and features
botanically correct flowers. On the sofa is a harmonizing patchwork of tulips. A tulip was centered
on each seat cushion and back section, as well as on the pillows. A green welt is the only detail
needed with a pattern this large.*

A sofa is often the focal point of the living room, and frequently the first article of furniture to be chosen, since it is a large and expensive item that can determine the style of, and budget for, the surrounding pieces. Some points to consider when buying a sofa are anchor, shape, style, form, function, and durability. This camelback sofa, by Michael Vanderbyl for Baker Furniture, has a silhouette that works in traditional or modern spaces. The gentle curve of the back is either accentuated or camouflaged by the choice of fabric.

a

b

c

a Clarence House's "Arche de Noe" is a novelty damask with a large-scale woven repeat pattern with varied animal and bird figures throughout. The challenge was to show as many of these figures as possible, while repeating them in obvious places and matching the pattern over sections as necessary. While in some cases it is considered important to match segments of the sofa's upholstery, here we chose to take some liberties in order to feature all the animals in the pattern. Although the seat cushion frame (front border) does not match the deck (the section directly above the legs), the overall effect is successful because of the playfulness of the fabric.

This textile is strong by virtue of both color and pattern, so our only embellishment was a small-scale self-welt. In this case, the self-welt also helps to disguise the unmatched pattern. This sofa offers a fine example of breaking the rules in regard to pattern matching.

b Because of their geometric appearance, plaids must match perfectly. Unfortunately, this is not always possible since most plaids vary by minute degrees on account of the weaving process. Stabilizing a plaid pattern by fusing it with another textile (knit-backing) can help, as can a process referred to as "double ending" during sewing. When two pieces of material are joined, a central point in the length is tacked first to ensure the match, followed by careful and slow sewing from the two opposing ends toward the middle tack. It should be noted that this solution is not always successful, and many manufacturers and suppliers of plaid textiles attach disclaimers that place limitations on pattern matching.

Our plaid sofa is clad in Osborne & Little's "Kashipur, Tilara," a semi-large-scale woven plaid with four dominant colors: white, tangerine, orange, and fuschia. As an embellishment, a bias-cut (candy-cane effect) welting was employed for graphic

punch, and the bolsters were produced by gathering the ends into a starburst, finished with a fabric-covered button.

c This sofa is covered in Scalamandré's "Chinese Disc." The pattern consists of two woven bands of circles, staggered with each other to produce an organized dot pattern. It is quite graphic, given the contrast between the melon and gold threads. The pattern was placed by railroading the fabric (running the fabric horizontally) to avoid creating seams. Simple self-welts, as well as a coordinating silk moss fringe on the bolsters, were utilized as embellishments. To create a uniform appearance, one row of circles placed on the border of the cushions was juxtaposed with the row on the frame below the cushions, mimicking the way the fabric is woven and upholstered on the sofa back.

d

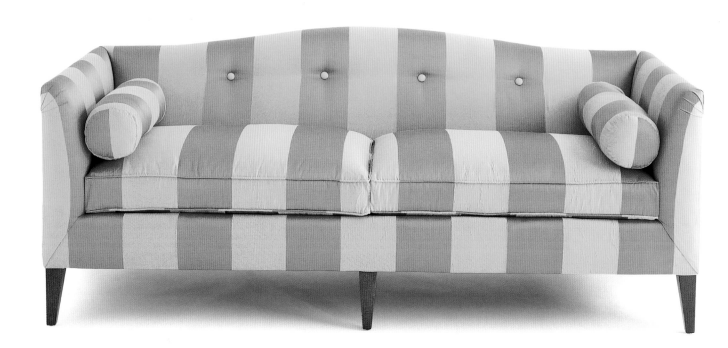

e

f

d Manuel Canovas' "Frederic II" is a striped velvet, and we ran it horizontally to elongate the sofa visually without any welting or embellishment. This is a much more modern statement than running the fabric in a waterfall, or vertical direction, and would work well in a space with particularly high ceilings or in a room whose proportions and other design elements can withstand such a break from the norm. The camelback of the sofa also takes on new life, since the stripes accentuate and exaggerate the scale of its height by showing two extra, albeit abbreviated, stripes from the bolt.

Perfect matching is of paramount importance here. When using a striped velvet, extra care must be taken so that all converging lines match with the coordinating "color" or weave of the velvet. By railroading the fabric, the perception of color change is muted and noticeable only upon careful side-to-side inspection. The bolsters for this sofa were manufactured by cutting pie-shaped pieces of the stripe so that the cut pile meets in the center of the bolster's circle, and a contrasting button was added as a finishing detail.

e This silk blend, Bergamo's Sahco Hesslein "Delicia," a simple alternating stripe of equidistant width, was woven to produce an iridescent orange and yellow fabric. We applied it in a straightforward and traditional way. The pattern match from each section of the upholstery—the back, the seat, the deck—to the next was crucial. We used welting on the cushions for definition and a pleated finish on top of the arms to allow the stripe to gracefully turn the edge to the outside arm without clumsily interrupting the pattern. Small fabric-covered buttons were used in a contrasting color within the stripes on the seat back as an unexpected embellishment, and the bolsters were cut to match their stripes to the arm of the sofa.

f "Sconset" from Brunschwig & Fils, a woven floral matelassé on a diamond-shaped grid, has one large and one small repeat following in an organized trellis across the fabric in a zigzag pattern. The key to the success of this upholstery is the uniformity of the pattern on each section of the sofa, as well as the organized match from section to section. Self-welting, cut on the bias from the same predominant red color, is used for detail.

Like many matelassé fabrics, this one is woven to be reversible, with the predominantly red face changing to white on the other side. To take advantage of one's ability to show this fabric from both sides, we reversed the face on the bolster pillows as well as on an arched pattern of buttons across the back of this sofa. Another popular way to utilize a reversible fabric such as this matelassé would be to employ it in reverse fashion on an accessory piece of furniture like an ottoman, or to cut a reverse section for the leading edge of a pair of curtains.

g

h

i

g In our treatment of this fabric, Schumacher's "Arabesque Taffeta," an extremely careful pattern match from all angles of the sofa was imperative, since the motif of the repeat is strong and singular, and any mistake would be obvious. As an embellishment, fabric-covered buttons tuft the two seat cushions to mimic the undulation of the flocking on the seat. A self-welt cut on the bias is sewn into seam allowances of the cushions and the bolsters, and careful consideration is given to the cut so that the pattern is correctly lined up on the circular ends of the bolsters.

h This embossed velvet, Quadrille's "Domino," is a fairly sturdy choice as velvets go, since a multitude of mistakes can be disguised within such a busy pattern.

The strength of the pattern allows us to use the fabric in a straightforward way, showcasing the grid and subtle color variations. As embellishment, tiny fabric-covered buttons, upholstered on the sofa back in a diamond motif, offer a counterpoint to the strict uniformity of the grid and draw attention to the raised camelback of the sofa. A simple self-welt, cut on the bias and wrapped around a smaller-scale welting cord (smaller cord is always preferable with heavier fabrics), is used on both the seat cushions and the bolster for linear definition of their forms.

i Crewel is usually a plain-weave fabric, most often (but not always) wool, embellished with chain stitch embroidery. It is available in a large variety of scales, color combinations, and qualities. Lee Jofa's "Jammu Crewel" has a tightly woven cotton background, with a red worsted wool chain stitch that shows a floral, leaf, and tendril motif. Given the large scale of the repeat, amid its multidirectional chain stitch, we were able to railroad the fabric and avoid seaming.

Because the pattern of this crewel is so broad and open, very little attention is required with regard to cutting and placement on the frame; again, mismatching adds to the handmade sensibility of the fabric. Nonetheless, in certain places (such as the arm faces and the bolster ends), careful pattern-matching makes sense and allows for some imposed order.

As our only embellishment, solid red linen has been used to welt the seat cushions, delineate the arm edges, and form a circular edge on the bolster. This solid welting adds definition to the shape of the sofa by working in opposition to the scattered and random effect of the pattern.

modern sheraton sofa

Dessin Fournir's "Dunning Sofa," with its elegantly slender seat back and arms, is a modern interpretation of the classic form of a Sheraton sofa, down to the whimsical faux brass caps on the carved and cantilevered legs. Comfortable to sit on as well as pleasant to look at, it blends the shape of the authentic Sheraton-style sofa, produced most notably in the first third of the nineteenth century in Salem, Massachusetts, but with more modern details.

This updated classic fits the bill in modern as well as traditional environments. Fabric choices can make its stately form appropriate for a modern loft or at home with authentic pieces from almost any period. As is evident in the simple white version, one look says style, and lots of it, and there are an endless number of ways to utilize this piece in interiors.

In its original setting this sofa would have been used for conversation on formal occasions, in special places in the home reserved for greeting guests, or entertaining family. As such, the comfort level may not be exactly what one would want in a casual family room. In reviewing our "Good, Better, Best" discussion (pages 192–195), it should be noted that this sofa is in a category of its own. The sparseness of proportion evident in all sections of this piece calls for specific infrastructural supports, and while the possibility of short-coil seat springs exists, it is more likely that a good quality zipper spring would be utilized on both seat and back to help minimize bulk.

(a)

(a) (b) (c) (d) (e) (f) (g)

Our fabric choices break down into three basic conceptual categories: rigid repeats, contemporary asymmetrical, and organized modern novelty. The two patterns that show rigid repeats are Scalamandré's "Begley" (a) and Rose Cumming's "Tangier Stripe" (b). These fabric choices, all in our chosen palette of brown, beige, and off-whites, have an imposed and regimented order seemingly well suited to the formal shape of this sofa. Sophisticated, these fabrics bring the sofa closer to its historical role in a formal room in the home.

(b)

c

In the contemporary asymmetrical category are "Sausalito," from Clarence House (c), "Chevron," from Dek Tillett (d), and "Botanique Crewel," from Stroheim & Romann (e). In contrast to the previous classification, this trio allows casualness and playfulness to be applied along strict guidelines, creating a balance between historical form and the modern home. Both the Sausalito and Botanique patterns are completely asymmetrical, making the eye seek out the contour beneath the print. Of the three, the Chevron, a modern printed interpretation of a traditional bargello (a needlework stitch that produces a zigzag pattern,

decorator's tips

- A room filled with boxy furniture begs for at least one shapely upholstered piece.

- Subtle patterns accentuate a piece's silhouette

- Stripes and prints liven up a prim and proper piece.

- Patterned fabrics need to be seamlessly matched when upholstered—it's worth the time and money to do it right.

- Center a fabric motif on accent pillows, or try reversing the fabric for contrast.

- "Less is more" is the rule when it comes to embellishing simple streamlined pieces.

d

named after the upholstery in the Bargello, a well-known Florentine museum), with its uneven pattern, is perhaps the most unusual. Experimenting with a radically different fabric on a very traditional sofa is one of the most interesting ways to push the design to its limits, and to achieve a successful yet unexpected result.

In the organized modern novelty series, we find KA International's "Natal" (f) and Designers Guild's "Vendome" (g). This duo of fabrics includes repeats scaled from the small to the oversized. Natal's tiny paisley, embroidered in a wide and loose repeat across a burlap ground, sets the tone for a middle ground—a slightly less dramatic divergence between sofa form and textile.

e

f

Two rectangular toss pillows have been added to each of our sofas, in each case carefully utilizing a particular section of the repeat; the ability of the textile to be used on its reverse side can make for a subtle change, or a simple moss fringe, cord, or ribbons can set the pillows apart from the background. The effect gained by this is an overall lightening of the sofa's basic form.

g

love seat

A love seat is built for two—often with style rather than comfort in mind. The name connotes an amorous respite, a seat for intimate conversations. These pieces of furniture are fashioned in a variety of styles, from every historical era, and can be made to play a part in any interior. The design without arms that we show here, the Dennis Kidney Loveseat from Brunschwig & Fils, conveys a more tranquil and casual atmosphere, suitable to a bedroom or small sitting nook, whereas pieces designed with arms are often included in formal "suite" arrangements. In a generously proportioned room, for example, two love seats might provide a second seating area placed off to one side.

Pink seemed an obvious choice for a love seat. Its many shades—from softest rose petal, through blush, coral, bubble gum, raspberry, fuschia, and near-purple—express everything from demure sexiness, to fun, wit, and outrageousness.

c

a An open field, white-ground cotton print, Osborne & Little's "Nanzen," features three different-hued overscaled roses as the motif, set against a gracefully cascading flurry of petals and leaves.

Perhaps the greatest challenge with a print of this nature is the placement of the repeat on the frame. The roses do not follow a regimented repeat, instead falling in a random way. By rolling the fabric over the love seat, we found that we could display all three of the roses. We chose the dark pink rose to center the back, seat, and skirt.

Minimal detailing as well as cautious sewing were also key. A simple coordinating grosgrain ribbon finish on the bottom of an inverted box-pleated skirt (carefully cut and sewn to allow the flowers to join over the pleat, while exposing the middle of the flower inside of the pleat) serves to "lift" or separate a white-grounded pattern from the floor. It is also practical, as it protects the fabric from becoming dirty.

b This composition, "Draperie" by Charles Burger, of raspberry and white, printed onto a trellis of swags, flowers, and playful architecture, also features numerous figures and birds—one of the hallmarks of a classic toile. This pattern evokes uniformity, balance, order, and wit, practically dictating the rhythmic placement of the pattern on the piece. Perhaps the greatest challenge is matching each of the lyrical motifs across the sections of this love seat to ensure continuity. Cautious planning—measure twice, cut once—is the rule here.

A scaled block fringe was attached to the bottom of the skirt, which was slightly ruched at two points on the front edge, to soften the formal effect of the trellis pattern. The fringe mimics the flirty swing of the print, as well as buffering the white-grounded fabric from the floor.

c Country Swedish's "Royal Salon," is a bright and cheerful silk check. We began with a plainly upholstered back and seat and added flourish with a shirred border, piped with self-welting for definition, running along the edge of the seat back. Five small fabric-covered buttons were placed in a pyramid design on the white sections of the check, echoing the shape of our love seat and indirectly calling attention to the widening skirt. One of our most feminine detailings, a lush, richly gathered skirt, lined in cotton for substance, makes this piece perfect for a private dressing room or for the foot of a bed.

d

f

This soft-hued, pink-and-white check, Brunschwig & Fils' "Antigua," comprises gentle, white, rope-like lines crisscrossing a pink field. Grids are a simple upholstery challenge with regard to placement and engineering, presenting themselves as preorganized and seemingly ready to be placed. The starting points were a straight upholstery treatment on the seat back and seat, punctuated by a bias welting. Then a full-circle, box-pleated, lined skirt was added, perfectly matching the grid on the seat by measuring pleats carefully. By railroading the fabric on the piece, we avoided seaming on the seat and back, and were able to cut the skirt from a running fabric edge to allow the tassel to form the border of the skirt. This allowed us to utilize an existing motif as an accent detail.

Two large white buttons draw attention to the seat back and add counterpoint to the skirt detail.

e This subtle print, Osborne & Little's "Wastra Blossom," mimics the scales of snakeskin and appears almost as a solid color. Since its simple mottled motif requires no matching, there were few problems to consider. The scales of the print are directional, so the upholstery was done in waterfall fashion, allowing the scales to fall top to bottom instead of side to side.

While myriad detailing possibilities exist—especially for a fabric with such a simple design—we chose only two, namely scallops and welting. The top line of the skirt has a border created with two rows of welting, two inches apart, to separate the seat from the skirt—a minor detail, but one that works well with an uncomplicated pattern. Even in pink, a snake print has an edginess so the scalloped skirt is the perfect element to add interest.

Note that the pleats are bisected by the center of a scallop: another example of an effectively executed detail. A single medium button punctuates the seat back.

f Any textile with an organized and repetitious pattern, like "Emma," by Cowtan & Tout, calls for straight-forward fabric placement.

For this piece, five solid medallions were placed on the inside back, accentuating the way the shape of the love seat broadens as it descends toward the floor. Simple self-welting, cut on the bias, borders the back and top of the skirt line. The skirt is pieced together in front from five separate sections, cut and positioned to be sewn back together so that the medallions match perfectly over the pleat openings, as well as uniformly exposing the smaller medallions within the pleat. Another simple addition to the skirt is a white strip of linen that has been pieced into the bottom of the skirt, two inches above the floor line, to form a border with the smaller medallions. The result, an organized and showy piece, was accomplished by careful planning, cutting, and placement. Note that this kind of tailored effect is often more difficult to produce successfully, as every detail can be seen so clearly.

g

h

i

^g The English interpretation of this upholstery is inspired by the chintz. This example, John Rosselli's "Ribbons," is a two-tone cascade of interlocking ribbons with a feminine sensibility.

We employed a coral-colored moss fringe on the edge of the back and as a border to the skirt in order to both soften them and add a tactile counterpoint to the polished cotton chintz. We ignored the pattern with regard to matching; the repeat is so busy and distracting that attempting to continue the lines of the ribbons seemed pointless. The top line of the skirt is piped with a raspberry-colored linen welt, without which the transition between the upholstery of the seat and the gathered edge of the skirt would become blurred.

These two distinct different uses of the fabric (stretched over the seat and back, then gathered for the skirt) are perfectly suitable for chintz because of its stiffness. The solid color moss fringe visually separates

the skirt from the floor, and forms a buffer against dirt. It also forces a change in the way the chintz (which would usually cascade straight to the floor) behaves, causing it to undulate at the edge. Sewing extra yardage into the bottom hemline of the gathered skirt creates the impression of a formal crinoline underskirt, billowing out the overskirt with lush extravagance.

^h This predominantly white ground embroidered fabric, Carleton V's "Bachelor Button," is soft and feminine. The flowers seem to float like balloons toward the sky. Because there is a clear repeat, we placed the fabric so that the stems would cascade over the top edge, bordered by a self-welt. This created a frame and revealed a pyramid pattern of flowers on the seat back, which echoes the way the piece widens toward the floor line.

First cut and then cautiously pieced back together (with seams hidden in the gathers), the skirt shows a row of floral bouquets

that contrast nicely with the scattered bunches on the tightly upholstered sections. The skirt also has two rows of grosgrain ribbon in slightly different shades of pink, sewn to the top of the skirt at a quarter the size of the larger ribbon sewn at the base. A gathering tape was applied to the reverse side directly below the top ribbon, and pulled to create the "flange" ruffle at the skirt's top edge.

ⁱ The most tailored and pared down of all the treatments, this fabric, Scalamandré's "Bermuda Cloth," is shown here with minimal detailing. Small-scale, single-welt cord adds to the minimalist effect by delineating the two edges of the seat back, as well as the top edge of the skirt, where it almost invisibly attaches to the base. A single center pleat in the skirt is barely visible but adds a touch of softness and detailing to balance the severely tailored treatment and to match the subtle femininity of the color.

family-size sofa

Bennison's "Bollington" sofa, generously proportioned with a classic shape, is the perfect perch for three adults; or two adults, two children, a bucket of popcorn, and a DVD.

Overscaled sofas often are seen through decidedly dark glasses by the design community, but as is evidenced here, style need not be compromised to accommodate a crowd. This is a sofa that will suit almost every decorating scheme—from traditional to modern. The stylishly turned front legs with brass casters lighten the piece's weight and scale. The straight carved back legs—almost standard on caster front sofas—add stability. A tight back (a great plus in an overscaled sofa, no fluffing and repositioning of the back cushions), three loose seat cushions filled with down and feather for the ultimate in comfort, two outwardly pitched arms, and two toss pillows to scrunch up behind the small of your back—all work in concert to create a silhouette that suits almost every decorating scheme.

As our fabric choices show, this sofa is extremely versatile; it can be dressed as easily for an afternoon matinée as for an evening opera. As we have noted, a sofa is usually the cornerstone or centerpiece of a room, and its scale, comfort, style, and choice of fabric will direct the use of the remaining space. This is especially true with a piece as large as this: the fabric chosen must be entirely suited to the purpose and design concept of the living space. If you have small children and pets, careful consideration of your textile is key.

a

a Because its repeat is small, this horizontal zigzag pattern—Robert Allen @ Home's "Hill and Dale" —was railroaded across the sofa's seat and back. We found a cotton broadcloth in the print's darkest hue for the pillows, which are trimmed in a pale pink linen, sewn with a half-inch fan-edge French knife pleat. The pleats echo the fabric's wavy pattern.

b Brunschwig & Fils' "Oh Susannah," a brightly colored chintz floral, is a stylishy fresh take on a traditional motif. We centered the white orchids of this summery pattern on each seat cushion and both arms. For pillows and welting we chose inexpensive lime-green linen.

b

c

c The repeat in this large-scale floral, "Kala" by Raoul Textiles, is slightly irregular. You must lay out the fabric on the sofa before choosing where to match the pattern. The tiny leaves are picked up in the pillows' jade green linen; the crisp welting on both the sofa and the pillows is in bright red linen.

d Bennison's "Dragon Flower" tree of life print is a decidedly upscale linen print featuring two large organic motifs, both of which are centered on the sofa's back. Because the print is so elaborate, there was no need to get matchy-matchy; the trim is self welt. A simple red linen on the pillows echoes the red in the print; the gold pom-pom trim repeats the fabric's circular swirls.

d

(e)

(e) We eyeballed this Kravet's check as it came off the bolt so that the dark blue stripe would run vertically, making the sofa look taller. The fabric—a simple midscale check—was cut on the bias for the welting and the pillows, which required extra yardage. An inch-wide, hot-pink raffia trim outlines the pillows.

(f) A solid fabric such as "Le Drap" by Manuel Canovas demands clever details to add interest. Two-inch-wide purple grosgrain ribbon was applied along the bottom of the frame; for the pillows, it was mitered and inset one inch. On the seat cushions, we folded the ribbon in half to make a flange trim. The arms have no welting, which makes for a clean look.

(f)

g

g This hand-blocked lattice print from John Robshaw is slightly irregular in color saturation, so we were careful to lay out the pattern evenly. To complement the fabric's soft, washed look, we used no welting. We trimmed the pillows in a half-inch looped brown raffia.

h The asymmetrical repeat of Donghia's "Espadrille" stripes did not fit the sofa's width evenly. To make it symmetrical, we cut the stripe and seamed it so that the pattern would line up in the center of the sofa back. To match the stripes, we flipped one side of the seam upside down to create a mirror image. For contrast, we ran the stripes vertically on the sofa back and horizontally on the cushion edges and pillows. To keep the look modern, we used no trim.

h

decorator's tips

- Before choosing fabrics for furniture that gets lots of wear and tear, think about cleanability. Many fabrics can be prewashed for easier spot-cleaning or fiber-sealed for stain resistance. Check with your upholsterer.

- While not one of our fabric choices here, "contract" or commercial grade fabric is often used by designers for family sofas. In recent years, the demand for more stylish and interesting fabrics within this category has skyrocketed, so this may be worth considering if your sofa is likely to see above-average wear and tear.

- To make horizontal furniture look taller, use fabrics with vertical patterns, and add contrasting pillows in corners to draw in the eye.

- Sofas with loose seat and back cushions are comfortable, but they tend to look sloppy after heavy usage. A sofa with a tight back and loose seat cushions can still be comfortable but has a neater look.

- Furniture on casters tends to be unsteady. To make sure your sofa doesn't move around, put skid pads under the legs or make sure the two front legs are resting on a carpet.

DETAILS

A sofa with a tight back—as opposed to one with pillows—looks sleek and contemporary. We ran China Seas' "Charade" polka-dot pattern across the seat and back, which saved yardage.

A single row of dots runs across all edges of the seat cushions and along the bottom line of the frame.

Solid brown linen welting along the seat and bottom edge of the frame anchors the busy pattern; we used the same linen on the pillows. Dark colors always pull the eye in on a horizontal piece.

To prevent your sofa from moving around on its casters, put skid pads under the legs or make sure the two front legs are resting on a carpet.

pillow-back sofa

With its simple lines, straightforward and elegant proportions, and uniform arm and back height, Hamilton Furniture's Henry sofa is perhaps the most versatile of all our sofas, at home both in traditional and contemporary settings. Choosing coral (a combination of red, white, and yellow) as a starting point, we set off to create as many variations in style as there are exhibited in this chameleon of colors.

At 76 inches in length, this sofa can accommodate three adults comfortably, and the six loose-back pillows (generously filled with down and feather) and one mattress-like seat cushion make it extremely versatile. It is always important to consider how your sofa will be used, and in what context, before choosing upholstery fabric and embellishments. The same sofa used in a seating area of a modern loft upholstered in Hable Construction's "Orange Beads" (b) would look equally well in a paneled room wearing Hinson's floral "Lutece" (i) trimmed in lush moss fringe. As we've emphasized here, it is the fabric choice that sets the stage for the ultimate style of the furniture piece, and leads us in different directions with regard to pattern placement, welting, and embellishments. Note also that in three examples (f, g, and i) we've used a skirt, while the sofa's legs are left bare in the other examples.

c

a John Robshaw's "Persian Rose" is a hand-blocked, cotton-ground print, with subtle variations in the spacing of the stylized floral medallion. This type of random repeat pattern—achieved by the cautious eye of the printer, who hand-blocks the pattern in a scattered fashion while attempting to achieve some amalgam of repeat—is the most difficult kind of fabric pattern for an upholsterer. The challenge here is to cut and arrange the pattern so that it is clear the print was designed to appear random while at the same time approaching some sort of visual unity. This is the one occasion where the rules of pattern matching can be ignored. Careful examination of the unrolled bolt of raw material is required, then cutting to maximize order—as is evident here in the border on the cushion and on the plinth directly below that. While the arms and

pillows don't reflect this order, it allows the final effect to be read as handmade. We used a white linen welt to help "return" the original shape to the sofa, and to introduce a little underpinning architecture to the pattern (as the ridged lines of the frame seem to call for).

b Hable Construction's "Orange Beads" takes a twenty-first century look at the application of a pattern with a retro 1960s feel: tiny orange circles, in slightly asymmetrical rows, on an off-white field. To break up the busyness of the bead pattern, we decided to upholster the frame with an unprinted ground fabric, and also to use it both as welting on the seat cushion and to delineate the six back pillows. The resulting interplay between the two different yet clearly related fabrics is fresh and modern.

c Also in a modern vein, Rogers & Goffigon's "Sanderling" is perfectly suited to our versatile frame. Its use of ordered stripes, matched perfectly from the back to the arms, cushion, and plinth, read like piano keys over the boxy frame. To break up the regimented stripe and add a whimsical note, the pillows on the back of this sofa have been cut and engineered to create two patterns: a series of interlocking squares and a "bull's-eye" cross.

d

e

f

d In a more traditional vein, Clarence House's "Tahiti," a stylized sea coral pattern, is woven to be reversible. We upholstered the sofa as cleanly as possible, without welting or other trims, taking full advantage of this reversible fabric, using the red side for the body and seat of the sofa, and the white side for the pillows. The pattern was laid out so that the coral motifs would be distributed symmetrically.

e Gaston y Daniela's "Egeo," a subtle tone-on-tone damask-inspired print, has one of the largest repeats used on this frame. Railroading a pattern that has a definitive vertical print is not an option. This pattern was carefully matched so that it would fall perfectly across the seat cushion and onto the frame. To give the subtle pattern a lift, we framed the central motif of the design (placed in the middle of each pillow) with a four-inch band of linen in a darker tone.

f Pierre Frey's "Contrefond Napoleon III" in coral and white, has a complicated and slightly over-scaled repeat of intricately drawn lattice and fretwork—another example of the need for cautious pattern placement and matching, as a mistake here would be an obvious eyesore. To rein in the strong pattern, welting in the darker red of the print was chosen to outline the entire ensemble. The addition of a skirt—either upholstered onto the frame as is shown here, or used as a seasonally changing slipcover—creates a completely different look and shows how versatile a frame of this simple shape can be. To gild the lily, a bias border of one of the overscaled lattice stripes was cut from the fall-off (the scraps that fall off as the fabric is cut) of the fabric and carefully rejoined to create a banding for the bottom edge of the skirt. The result is a sofa perfectly suited to a formal setting.

g

h

i

g To give this lighthearted chinoiserie print ("Shangrila" by Summer Hill) a hint of formality, a kick-pleated skirt trimmed with black bullion fringe was added and each pillow was surrounded with black pom-pom fringe. Simple self-welting appears everywhere else.

h Cowtan & Tout's "Fairmont" required careful placement because the riders on this equestrian print are trotting in opposite directions. Half the pillows feature one rider at the center and half the other rider. Faux-suede welting in taupe furthers the sporting theme.

i The pattern of this traditional floral print—Hinson's "Lutece"— was matched from the seat cushion down to the floor, but the variety of flowers meanders across the frame. A different flower shows its face on each pillow, which is trimmed with off-white cotton moss fringe. Elsewhere, self-welting was used.

decorator's tips

- A clean-lined sofa like this one is a great investment because it can work in either a modern or traditional setting.

- This sofa looks more contemporary if you expose its great legs. If you like the traditional look of a skirt and want your sofa to do double duty, try adding a skirted slipcover.

- Reversible fabrics are fun to experiment with, but before you act, double-check with your supplier or upholsterer to make sure the material is truly intended for reversing.

- Although hand-blocked prints are beautiful, they often lack perfectly repeating patterns. When working with such a fabric, lay it out on the piece before you cut it to distribute the design evenly.

high-backed settee

Mitchell Gold's Carter Settee is loosely based on a Sheraton-style wing chair of the nineteenth century (with turned legs rather than the ball-and-claw of the Chippendale version) and offers perfect seating for two. The settee's simple and elegant form lends itself to striped fabrics, the variety of which—from tone-on-tone single colors, to elaborately woven damasks with stripes carefully hidden within pineapples and pomegranates—allows for a range of tastes unavailable in any other category of pattern. This piece of furniture illustrates a general truth that the better thought out the original silhouette, the easier it is to widen the range of fabric choices.

We chose stripe patterns that have a variety of fiber contents, widths, and weaving techniques, but correspond to the definition of stripe. The only real departure from traditional stripes to be noted within the ranks of our fabric choices are the asymmetrically designed stripes, which do not follow an exact order across the width of the finished material, calling for re-engineering to produce a successfully upholstered settee.

Height was one of our primary considerations with this piece, because the high back allows us to consider running the stripes horizontally across the frame for a fresh and unexpected finish.

a Mulberry's "Old School Stripe" has beautiful colors, a strong visual rhythm, and the serendipitous possibility of using a single stripe on the armband and as an embellishment across the bottom of the frame, eliminating welting. The problem that this fabric presented is that its weave is a "continuum repeat"; that is, one stripe follows another without ever stopping to reverse itself, and thus the pattern lacks a natural symmetry. This can be a problem on upholstered pieces and window treatments, since the eye expects the stripe to reverse itself on center, so that the settee begins and ends on the same color stripe. A simple solution is to cut and rejoin it in the center of the settee, one half upside right, the other upside down, so as to organize the stripe into a mirror image of itself.

b Another selection in the vertical category is Ralph Lauren's bold, modern "Fisher's Island Stripe." We again avoided welting for fear of blurring the crisp and calculated juxtaposition of wide to narrow stripes. But not wanting to err on the side of blandness, we ran the stripe horizontally across the arms of the settee (with the added advantage of not wasting fabric left as fall-off). This also draws the eye subliminally toward the piece, inviting one to sit and relax.

c

d

c Two very different results are achieved by running the stripes horizontally. With Clarence House's "Marina Stripe," the stripe emphasizes the settee's oversize wing chair shape. By virtue of the strength and scale of the repeat, we see a stream-lined horizontal stripe, and eight different colors repeated on a sub-dued cream border. The fabric is carefully matched from the back to the wings, and punctuated by a thin yet defining cream welt. The technique of using a solid welt succeeds especially with this thin stripe, as it allows the eye to move between the flowing horizontals and the definitions the solid outline affords.

d The second example of horizontally employed fabrics is Toiles du Soleil's "Lulu" circus stripe. Modern and witty, the pattern is cut so that the fabric flows from the top to the bottom of the frame without interruption. The arm caps have been cut from the tomato-colored stripe in order to refocus attention on the settee's original shape. Yellow welting contrasts with the predominant red, and adds further charm to this unexpected fabric.

e

f

e No tricks were needed with
this classic English drawing-room
stripe, "Hadrien" by Manuel
Canovas. The colors give it the
kick. Ivory Ultrasuede trim outlines
the shape and provides a visual
break from the strong hues.

f "Jamboree" by Mitchell Gold,
a big blowup of a man's shirting
stripe, was handled in simple classic
style. The stripes run vertically;
bias-cut self-welting finishes the
edges of the arms and seat cushion.

g

h

g Because "Neva" by Bergamo is an asymmetrical stripe in velvet, we could not cut and reengineer it to center the stripes. The three pale stripes along the back and the arms are spaced unevenly, but the strong pattern camouflages the variations.

h We ran this "bar code" stripe— "Sarawak" by Thomas Dare— horizontally across the entire piece. The busy lines are controlled by red welting that matches the darkest red of the stripe.

decorator's tips

- Stripes can be asymmetrical or symmetrical. However, for most fabrics, it is possible to cut and refit them so that they can be centered on a piece of furniture.

- If you want to widen or soften the lines of a piece, "railroad" the fabric horizontally. If you want the appearance of greater height and a more classic look, "waterfall" the fabric vertically.

- Welting is normally cut on the bias, but with a striped fabric you can end up with a candy-cane effect—a potential disaster. You may want to consider using a solid-color welting instead.

- Save money on borders by cutting out one of the fabric stripes and using it as a trim.

DETAILS

"Narneanisha," a cotton chenille by Osborne & Little, is classic in weaving style but modern in color interpretation. It has a perfectly symmetrical mirror repeat pattern, returning to a central red stripe after a succession of turquoise, mustard, black, and white stripes.

The strength of the red stripe is utilized for the ridge on the arm and the center of the settee's "spine."

The bright colors and varying widths of the stripes inspired us to experiment. We ran the seat's stripes perpendicular to that of the frame with the same predominant red stripe featured as the box border of the cushion. The resulting crossing effect of the fabrics is unexpected, but in general seems to play well with the vibrant and witty colors chosen for the weave.

So as not to end up overmanipulating the stripe, an alternate fabric was used for welting. Black denim, cut on the bias, echoes the black stripe in the base fabric and gives crisp and weighty edges to the original form; this allows the settee's curve and stature to predominate and makes for an exuberant choice.

regency revival chaise

The "Lord Byron" chaise by Rose Tarlow for Melrose House is a Regency revival style recamier. With its sleigh shape and narrow profile, this daringly stylish piece of furniture is not for the faint of heart, although it could be successfully used as an accent piece in a generally quieter and more utilitarian collection of furnishings. Perhaps the best use for this uniquely shaped and designed chaise would be in a grand room among traditional pieces from varied historical eras. But it is also true that this piece could be the cornerstone of a studio apartment. As always, fabric choice is the key to ultimately successful positioning.

This chaise presents only two possibilities with regard to upholstery detailing, namely, the scrolled head and footboard. The head provides an opportunity for variation: depending on the fabric, a pleated edge can be upholstered on the head and foot edge or a more contemporary "panel" sewn to the base border. The sole chance to personalize the chaise and the fabric chosen is found in its one large pillow.

a

b

c

d

a **b** In a bid for contemporary glamour, we chose nine tones of gold to suit the chaise's shape. Two fabrics sporting geometric repeats needed to be treated in a straightforward manner, with flat panels on the arm and foot rest so that the pattern would not get lost in a series of pleats. The gold-and-white ikat "Nimes Check" from Cowtan & Tout (a), and the satiny "Agrabah" from Travers (b), are both for the most part squares upon squares. These shapes, if carefully cut to match along the edge of the frame, flow almost seamlessly from the top of one curve to the tip of the other. Single welting cut on the bias from the fabric itself outlines the arm and foot panels, adding definition to the shape. Dressmaker's details adorn the pillows on these chaises: a separate "flange" of fabric cut from the stronger gold color acting as a picture frame on the ikat check, and a

cascading French knife pleat, handmade and sewn carefully into the selvage of the Agrabah satin check.

c In full glamour mode is the aptly named "Grandeur" from Bergamo (c), with its outlandish damask repeat pattern in contrasting gold and white. This is the kind of fabric that demands the upholsterer, and possibly an interior designer, or perhaps even the client, spend time carefully mapping out the placement of the pattern. Note how the repeat is on such a grand scale that it appears almost not to repeat at all, and each area of the chaise shows off a unique motif. This is not by any means happenstance, but a result of planning, and the effect makes it look as though the fabric were designed and printed solely for this frame. Since the fabric is so extravagant, we trimmed the pillow in simple gold cord.

d **e** **f** **g** The remaining six golds are all upholstered with pleated arms, some intricate and gathered, and some more casually spaced, depending on the repeat of the pattern. The simplicity of Donghia's "Bindi" (f), the diminutive repeat of "Fiore Tresor" from Christopher Hyland, Inc. (e), along with the outlandish and unexpected nature of Stroheim & Romann's "Lindy Hop Figured Woven" (d) all lend themselves to extra pleating. The latter pattern in particular illustrates how the careful choice of color and a creative eye can marry two totally diverse concepts, such as a historically oriented frame and a whimsically drawn modern crafts pattern to produce one sensational finished product.

"Venice Silk" from Hinson & Co. (g), an alternating-width stripe in golden hues, is masterfully suited for a frame that sports both straight lines and gracious curves.

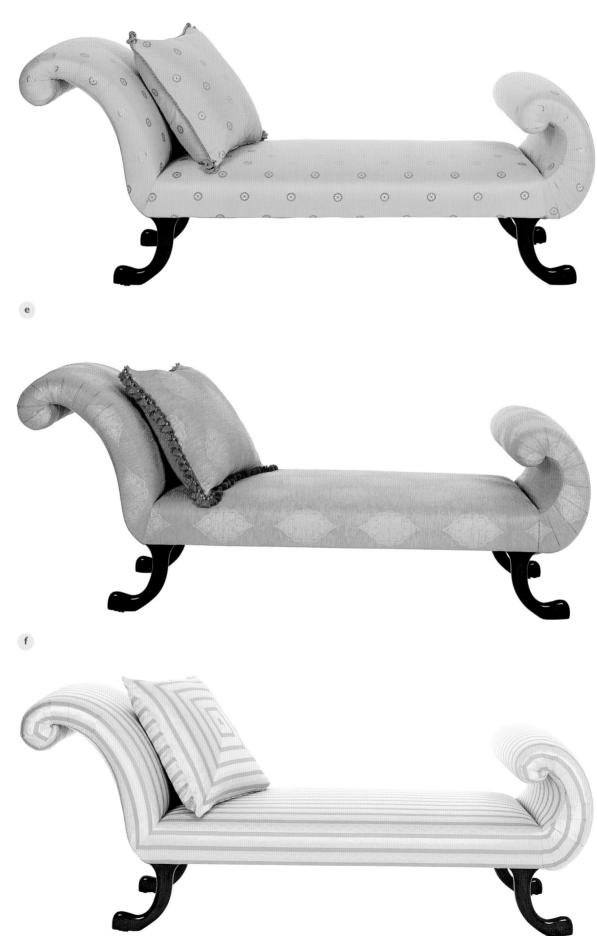

e

f

g

h

i

The manner in which the stripes ascend the arm and foot rest, slowly and effortlessly ending in subtle curved points, is the perfect counterpoint to the neatly designed pillow with the fabric cut on the diagonal and mitered.

h A playful embellishment on Osborne & Little's "Leontes" (h) with its silken circles of damask gold, is a double row of equally chic gold thread pompom fringe on the pillow.

i Finally, Fonthill's "Lola" (i), a striking matte-finished cotton print reminiscent of Moroccan tilework, is given an equally thick and lush moss fringe on its pillow, for what is probably the most casual looking of our treatments here.

Above: When Sweden's King Gustav III visited the court of Louis XVI at Versailles, he imported elements of the French neo-Classical decorative motif, notably oval-backed chairs and bateau-shaped sofas. Here, the blue-and-white upholstery is a typical Gustavian style, with a small print on a white ground.

Opposite: A mix of colorful prints with similar hues come together in this living room. On the sofa, a pattern with a large repeat that was centered on each pillow back and each seat. The trim along the bottom of the skirt prevents the carpet and the upholstery from blending together. An upholstered armchair (foreground) is draped with a bolt of petunia-motif fabric, while two opposite-facing chairs are covered in an intricate, but restrained, floral pattern.

Above: *Patterned pillows and a Persian-inspired textile draped casually on a cushion enliven an otherwise sober sofa fabric. Pillow designs are echoed in the subjects of the framed artwork.*

Opposite: *An elegant, curvaceous recamier, perfect for reading or napping, fills a sunny alcove in an otherwise spare and modern interior. The textile's stripes accentuate the recamier's sinuous forms. Details include a red trim on the frame, seat cushion, and bolster, and pleats around the curve of the seat back.*

The pillow reads: GUESTS OF GUESTS MAY NOT BRING GUESTS

Opposite: *Earth tones prevail in a room where furniture fabrics, throw pillows, window trim, and ceiling beams complement one another. Of particular note, the stripes on the sofa relate in scale and tone to the ceiling.*

Above: *Clean lines and muted hues combine in an outdoor room that remains protected from the elements. Red welting outlines sofa cushions and an ottoman; a conspicuous striping along the sides evokes plant greenery. A Moorish-style stained-glass lantern casts evocative mood lighting.*

Opposite, above: *Pillow-back sofas need not require that all cushions match, but it is important that fabric stripes align. Self-welting was used to trim the seat cushion and arms of the sofa.*

Opposite, below: *On a soft, casual sofa meant for sinking into, the striped pattern becomes more organic; matching throw pillows can be arranged according to whim. A narrower stripe is used for the back cushion of a wicker armchair.*

Above: *In some interiors, a sofa, such as this classic recamier, can double as a piece of sculpture—albeit a practical, comfortable one meant to be occupied. A plush, green velvet fabric makes for an elegant furnishing. Small nailheads provide visual and textural detail.*

Opposite: A faux tiger print is used to star-
tling effect on a pair of formal chairs whose
arms rest on tapering turned columns. A
tamer, luxurious bounty of flora appears on
the sofa and curtains, which are further
emphasized by hanging swags and fringe trim.

Above: The right fabrics can make an alcove
seem like a separate room. A red plaid statement on the wall, lampshades, sofa, throw
pillows, and nearby armchair, invites sitters. The
pillows feature a red-and-white trim evocative
of candy canes.

Opposite: *In this drawing room, part of a master bedroom suite, the avian motif is reiterated by matching Bird of Paradise wallpaper and chintz. A fanciful red fringe on the sofa contrasts with the precise, tailored lines of the skirt on an armchair.*

Above: *In this room, taking time to see the flowers means discovering that the same pattern is used on the walls and window shades as that on the sofa except that the backgrounds are different hues. Pillows, which match the wall coverings exactly, are trimmed with alternating gold and green tassels.*

Opposite: *The classic Swedish-inspired interior is defined by simple patterns, bleached surfaces, and bright, unadorned expanses. In typical Swedish style, the sofa, set on seven tapered legs, is covered with a delicate, white ground floral set within a white frame. In a room of hard surfaces, fabric stands out.*

Above: *The floral textile used on this sofa has a strong pattern, so the only embellishment used is the fringe on the pillows. A large-scale repeat, the pattern was not matched from section to section. Self-welting helps the motif blend from one piece to the next.*

chairs

The chair is the most fundamental piece of furniture in our lives. And its form is constantly being reexamined and reinvented. It seems that there is always a new way to sit. We can be comfortable in chairs with or without arms that are backless or three-sided, curved or rigid, unadorned or covered in plush fabrics. Chairs we choose for the home determine much about how we spend our daily lives.

Sitting pretty in a large-repeat toile requires positioning the material to reveal as much pattern as possible. Here, a virtual narrative is told on a wing chair precisely outlined by black welting. Whose profile is handsomer, that of one of the framed sitters or the chair's?

club chair

The club chair's shape is based on a classic mid-nineteenth-century design found in English country houses. It is as comfortable as it is beautiful. Elegant arms scroll graciously to the wide T-shaped seat cushion edge, following the natural contour of the resting arm in repose. With its extra-deep cushion, and perfectly pitched, tightly upholstered back, this is a time-tested example of classic form. Our example here, the George Smith Standard Chair, is considered by many designers to be the benchmark of both comfort and luxury.

Within the "Good, Better, Best" categories, discussed on pages 192–195 this chair most assuredly falls into "Best." Handmade, with the finest internal supports of boar hair, coil springs, and down cushion inserts, it should last as long as any antique, and can be reinvented with fresh upholstery as the years go by. With a frame as recognizable as this, restraint is called for: the chair's design should remain unadorned by skirts or decorative trimmings. Occasional nailheads at the chair's bottom line or simple self-welting or solid color-contrasting cord are acceptable, but more fanciful decoration will only detract from the classic silhouette.

a

a **b** The palette of fabrics chosen to show off our blue-ribbon frame were all drawn from the garden in a fitting homage to a British standard. The two palest fabrics, whose repeats are small and widely spaced, are "Francis Perry" from Carleton V (a), and "Concoran" from Steven Harsey Textiles (b). Both have white fields with loosely spaced, diminutive prints. The latter is a crewel stitch on raw silk, and as with most crewels, the motifs of this garden are connected by a vine-like trellis joining leaf to flower. Although the look is slightly more sophisticated than the delicate floral elegance of "Frances Perry," both remain soft and casual by virtue of the white ground.

c

d

c **d** In contrast, we utilized two fabrics with large-scale repeat patterns. Cowtan & Tout's "Botanique Spectaculaire" (c) has a monochromatic palette of blues set against a pure white background; and Rose Cumming's "Carisbrook" (d) features a soft polychromatic garden in shades from gray to burgundy set against a white-ground polished cotton (also known as glazed chintz). Both these fabrics make stronger statements than the previously discussed smaller repeat patterns but continue to possess a lighter sensibility because of their white grounds.

It should be noted that when the upholstery is without a great deal of embellishment, one must pay more attention to the process of aligning the pattern on the frame. Consider the large central flower centered on the seat back of both these chairs: it unerringly sets the pace and placement of the pattern for the entire piece. Each section of the chair (consider the cushion border in relation to the chair base) should match perfectly with the next so that the flowers appear to be growing across the planes of the chair. This requires caution in cutting and adding a predetermined seam allowance for sewing where necessary.

e

e f In sharp contrast to the light background and small repeat, both "Greta" from Sandberg (e) and "Opium Poppy" from Robert Kime (f) offer large-scale patterns. "Greta," with its scattered, asymmetrical arrangement of predominantly large florals on a tobacco-colored field, has been placed on the formal frame in a random fashion for a fresh and witty effect. Robert Kime's over-scaled pattern of red poppy and underlying ribbon on a cream-colored ground are not exactly sym-metrical, but do allow for the luxury of pattern placement, which gives the chair a sense of balance. An insider's tip: When a print like this one has large, repetitive sections of mostly dark color, a useful way to consider placing it on the chair's section is to "squint" so that you see the fabric's pattern as contrasting sections of light and dark.

Understanding the sections' proportions generally sets the ball rolling as to how best to upholster the frame. Subtle differences on the finished chair are inevitable with a pattern such as this (the arms here do not have exactly the same floral placement), but as in the landscapes from which these prints draw their inspiration, per-fect symmetry is often frowned upon by the experienced gardener, and the occasional encroachment of the vine upon the path could be considered serendipitous.

f

g

g Finally, Quadrille's floral pattern shows how a pattern with multiple elements (here vines, flowers, and stylized ribbons) can be a successful choice for this kind of chair. We considered allowing the ribbons to fall directly over the center of the chair, but decided that a better option would be to center the floral section of the pattern, and then allow the fabric to fall where it may. Perhaps the most successful of the group, this finished chair pairs a classic form with an untraditional, disorganized, and charming fabric—a perfect blend of tension and ease.

decorator's tips

- Notice how the color, scale, and density of a pattern changes the character of the chair. Prints on colored grounds give the chair more weight, whereas prints on light grounds give the chair a lighter look.

- Club chairs are often upholstered in leather, velvet, or kilim rugs, creating a masculine feeling. Here, a more feminine approach was taken by using floral fabrics.

- Elaborate trims would be too showy for this chair. Simple self-welting or solid color-contrasting cord offer just the right edging.

h

i

h **i** Some patterns don't require complex engineering. "Grayswood," an allover airy floral from George Smith (h), and "Samakand," in pink and green from Hinson (i), are two such examples, although care was taken to match the pattern from the seat cushion to the chair base.

wing chair

This classic wing chair, Michael S. Smith's Kelly chair with African-inspired turned-wood legs, was upholstered with paisley fabrics from many countries. The ornate fabric with its curved-teardrop pattern had its origins in India, where these abstract designs were most often used in cashmere shawls. Paisley soon found its way to Europe, becoming all the rage at the French court, then re-emerging in the simple cotton prints of the south of France. The motif eventually took its name from Paisley, Scotland, where shawls were woven from local wools.

Any print which incorporates the motif can be called a paisley, so the design travels the globe with regard to color palette, scale, position of stripes, checks, or squares, and repeats within contrasting patterns. From Kathryn Ireland's "Quilt," where the legendary motif is allowed to stand alone on a red background field alongside the occasional stylized dahlia, to Christopher Hyland's "Punjab Paisley" blissfully adrift in a sea of color with an over-lapping motif of monumental scale, clearly the sky is the limit.

a Perhaps the purest example of the traditional paisley shape is evident on "Giardino Paisley" from Quadrille. Here, a single overscale paisley motif is repeated within a solid, open field of blue. The paisley shape itself is ornate and highly stylized and is perfectly showcased here with a single row of green gimp—the color green drawn from within the printed paisley—to edge the bottom of the chair's frame, just above the legs. This serves to punctuate the end of the upholstery and the beginning of the contrasting turned legs which support the chair.

b Here is another example of paisley upholstered in a straightforward manner. Kathryn Ireland's "Quilt" has almost even proportions of red ground to print and no apparent direction. Again, the chair is upholstered in a straightforward manner with single welted cushion edges and nailheads as the finish of choice for the frame to leg edge.

DETAILS

"Moghul Paisley-Red" from Ralph Lauren Home is a sharp contrast to the other paisley prints shown here. Tiny paisley motifs abound in a design drawn from historical documents, ultimately comprising a large central medallion central to the width of fabric.

No great feats of upholstery are required—a central medallion is placed in both the center of the chair's inside back and on the center of the seat's loose cushion. When the repeat is of such large and demonstrative scale, the only logical thing to do is allow the pattern to dictate its continuation onto the adjoining planes of the chair.

As a variation on the double row of nailheads as a chair border detail, we used faux leather nailheads in a coordinating red to frame the base, with a space allowed between each nailhead.

c

d

c   Etro's "Azara," a paisley print within a stripe, was cut and resewn, or "engineered," in order to complement the fabric to the chair. This paisley print was upholstered horizontally. The inside edges of the wings have been carefully cut to match the pattern as it rounds the corner from the seat back with the surprise of a single stripe, cut and re-sewn on the inside wing panel, as a counterpoint to the horizontal lines and a subtle reminder of the chair's tall back.

d   Also engineered, the "Srinagar" chintz from Grey Watkins is also upholstered vertically and also introduces a stripe. As with the Etro print, a single band is cut and resewn to the inside wing section so that the line of the arm flows uninterruptedly from top to bottom. This fabric offers a twist of its own, showing paisley vertically in the overscale run and horizontally on a smaller scale, all set within a series of varying width stripes. It's a tour de force of design creativity, upholstered with minimum detailing so as to showcase the opulent fabric.

e

f

e Two of our patterns have "spines," or inherent vertical lines in the repeat, from which both sides show mirror images. The only questions are which spine to center, and how to orient the fabric. "Kashmir Paisley," from Stroheim & Romann, has several spines across the width of the fabric if run vertically. Our twist on the obvious is to run the fabric horizontally and find a second subliminal spine which dissects the print in a completely different way. Note how the mirror half of the pattern on the cushion border is matched to its twin on the chair's bottom frame, so that a straight line can be drawn up over the seat through the center of the four paisley tail hooks, dividing the back into a mirror image. As is often the case, it was essential here to have the original bolt of fabric to examine for the orientation of the fabric.

f The second "spined" fabric, Borderline's "Juniper," requires a choice of the lighter or darker segment of the print as center. We chose the bolder, lighter color as center, which along with the vertical stripe draws attention to the height of the chair.

g

h

decorator's tips

- Roll a few yards of a paisley fabric off the bolt and experiment with placement of the design motifs.

- Contemporary paisleys come in both prints and wovens.

- Vertical patterns make a chair seem taller; horizontal patterns shorten it.

- Remember that the front of the seat cushion and the plinth below it read together, so position your pattern accordingly.

- To complement paisleys, use nailheads in one of the several finishes and patterns, closely or widely spaced, in single or double rows.

- Try an unexpectedly modern paisley on a traditional chair.

g h These last two paisleys have much in common, both by virtue of their varied coloration as well as by the outer limits of large scale they represent. These combinations, in concert with our chair frame, offer a great chance for creativity and the opportunity to create a one-of-a-kind chair. "Punjab Paisley," from Christopher Hyland (g), incorporates a vast array of colors as well as repeats within the paisley motif. We cut and basted this fabric together to create our own version, with almost every section of the chair displaying a unique portion of the original repeat. With less variety in pattern but equal options in colors, "Cashmere Shawl" from Schumacher (h) is printed in a fairly uniform fashion. Because the fabric's print is set within a grid of sequential squares, we were able to cut and resew the colors in a pattern different to that of the original fabric. When rolled off the bolt, this fabric seems best suited to curtains. However, we reengineered the print to showcase all the possible colors on one chair, creating a totally unique look.

solo armchair

In the case of this chair, provenance is obvious: Italian at first sight. This chair was designed in 1999 by Antonio Citterio for B&B Italia. This design firm generally chooses to outfit its own furniture in solid materials from leather to wool and other plain fabrics. This piece is severe and rectilinear with a ribbon-thin base of chrome. Our selection of prints was therefore somewhat shocking, but we found a fresh way to look at a contemporary classic by working with a palette of blue and white, and several geometric patterns. To keep the chair's architectural style, we used clearly delineated patterns and no welting, fringes, tufting, or other embellishments. To be successfully upholstered in a print, this frame needed to have the underlying bone structure respected; when a clearly English or French pattern was utilized, we chose prints with hints of architectural detail, or if organic, those with a sense of order and regimentation.

a

b

c

a No exercise in true contrast would be complete without the utterly unexpected—within parameters that allow the frame to stand out. Looking first at the prints, which truly are surprises for this Italian cube, Jab's "Santa Ponza" is a wide-open crewel with blue embroidery on stark white cotton. This lyrical crewel adds a feminine touch to the chair's masculine form. The fabric leaves so much of the field unprinted that even with its vinelike repeat of leaves and strawberries, the frame and shape of the chair are totally evident.

b "Floating Lotus" from Hable Construction has loosely scattered, stylized lotus blossoms: B&B Italia goes to Palm Beach. Because the chair has a strong silhouette, the shape does not get lost in this witty print. We added a crisp navy-blue border to the box edge pillows to make them stand out.

c "Pavel" from Country Swedish, is a print of beautifully drawn seashells forming an organized repeat; the circles of the shells contrast with the square frame. The subliminal horizontal stripe, which can be seen with a slight squint of the eye, lines up beautifully on the frame—another somewhat surprising success. Grosgrain ribbon in two different tones of blue is mitered and inset in squares on the pillows.

d

e

CHAIRS

f

d Daring to choose a toile, "Willow" from Christopher Hyland may have been the farthest out on a limb that we ventured in terms of the aesthetics of chair and fabric. Have a closer look to understand the choice. While the exquisitely drawn motif is loose and scattered freely, within the hills and highly stylized trees are boldly set buildings of varying style as well as pagodas matching the architectural lines of the chair. The busy pattern allowed us to let the motifs fall somewhat randomly.

e Here is a handsome geometric motif that works successfully with the angles of the piece. In "Lighthouse Stripe" from Ralph Lauren Classics, a simple wide stripe was railroaded to run the stripes horizontally. The textile and chair are in perfect harmony because the grand navy-and-white stripe rolls off the bolt horizontally and lines up ideally on the frame—no seams needed.

f Pierre Frey's "Montfort," an ikat stripe, was waterfalled over the chair to give the frame some height and has the unexpected and stylish mitering of the print into squares on the cushions.

decorator's tips

- Not every piece of furniture works with a playful treatment, so choose wisely.

- If you take a risk with an exotic or vivid textile, do not take a risk with the trim, too.

- The simple blue-and-white color palette harmonized with the chrome frame and didn't overwhelm the chair.

- Try ribbon trim that complements but doesn't exactly match your fabric. It can provide the extra kick your pattern may need.

g

g Rounding out this group, "Tiki" from Scalamandré, the darkest and most saturated of the prints, has a check pattern. The checks were carefully lined up so that each stripe was strategically placed, especially at the edges of the seat and the center of the arms. The sole nod to whimsy was running the fabric in the opposite direction around the pillow's border.

h "Petite Zig Zag" from China Seas shows herringbone stripes created by the overlapping of delicate blue and white zigzags; a balanced and orderly design that is also appropriate and pretty on this chair. The pillow fabric was cut on the bias, and white linen was used for the box border as an echo of the chrome frame.

h

slipcovers

Slipcovers can instantly change the ambience of an entire room. They have an incredible array of uses: from concealing a heavier winter fabric upholstered to the frame, to darkening a light, summery fabric, to cheering up or dressing down for an occasion or an entire season. If you are buying custom furniture, consult with the manufacturer or representative—or directly with your designer—to see if it's possible to have a slipcover made while the furniture is being fabricated. This saves the time and expense of choosing a second fabric later, moving the piece back to the upholsterer, and waiting for the final slipcovers to arrive. In most cases a pattern can be cut from a lining cloth or muslin. Once the pattern is cut and the slipcover carefully fitted, the pattern can stay neatly folded in a dresser drawer waiting for the next change of outfit.

Slipcovers date back many centuries, often covering furniture that was upholstered in the finest silk and precious metallic threads (fabric that was usually more expensive than the wooden frame and labor cost combined) and removed only on special occasions. Today, with an array of available fabrics geared to every budget, slipcovers make more sense than ever and make possible in a matter of minutes the transformation of a room. Imagine a white dining room with a neutral rug and eight chairs of dark brown wood upholstered in taupe chenille. Then picture the same room with any of the nine slipcovers we've produced, and the room is reinvented by the simple act of applying the covers and pulling up the dressmaker zipper. Our chair, Thomasville's Alice B. sidechair, is an ideal candidate for a slipcover.

As with every transformation, however, creativity and attention to detail must be brought to bear on the chosen fabric in order to understand what possibilities exist. This is where the veteran upholsterer is important, as well as a design professional, since their eyes are trained to find the most beautiful way to assimilate the fabric, details, and the wishes of the client. The casual, slightly overscale slipcover may have its place, but our slipcovers are all well fitted and carefully tailored. The finished look is that of couture: each slipcover is individually designed and cut, and meticulous attention is paid to detail. With dressmaker flourishes or the restrained hand of the minimalist, the possibilities are endless. A truly well made slipcover looks like upholstery.

a

c

b

a To complement the pink-and-green "La Musardiere" toile from Manuel Canovas, we designed a feminine slipcover with a long, gathered skirt and a French-pleated hem. Rosy pink piping adds the finishing touch.

b On "Florizel" by Liberty, a charming summer-dress print, we scalloped the hem and outlined it in yellow linen. The slipcover's double corner pleats overlap like petals.

c To give Nya Nordiska's classic "Kappa-Check" an edge, we dressed it in a skirt with deep corner pleats and sexy corset lacing. The back, seat, and skirt sections of the slipcover were made with two inverted pleats down the center. We stitched down each pleat to make a flap and inserted a grommet on every other check. Crisp white grosgrain ribbon was used for the lacing.

d

f

e

d A modern take on a Chinese toile, Nina Campbell's "Manchu" inspired us to create a minimal slipcover with a short skirt, clean lines, and contemporary details. Each corner has two brass grommets with brown grosgrain ribbon ties. We inverted the ties and hid the ends under the hem to keep the look tailored. Note the expert pattern matching at the seat edges.

e To give a jolt in scale to Waverly's "Tavern Ticking" stripe, we cut and mitered 1½-inch grosgrain ribbon and stitched it in squares on the seat and back of the slipcover and as a band around the seat. To echo the squares, we added a straight skirt and notched the hem into 4 x 4-inch flaps edged with ribbon.

f With Marvic Textiles' "Toile de Chine," we placed the largest motif in the center of the seat panel. The sizable pattern repeat allowed us to place each additional motif strategically and to design a simple slipcover to show off the detailed drawings. The long skirt has kick pleats at each corner; covered buttons secure six bows to the seat and back.

CHAIRS

g

h

decorator's tips

- Why use slipcovers? To change the look of your pieces seasonally, to protect fine furniture, or just for fun.

- A simply shaped piece offers the largest number of possibilities for adding slipcover details.

- If you plan to wash your slipcovers, before cutting the pattern prewash the fabric: twice in hot water, twice in the dryer. Commercial dry cleaners also perform this service.

- Fabrics that work best for slipcovers are made of natural fibers: sturdy but lightweight cottons, linens, and wools. Easy to clean is the rule.

- When you think slipcovers, don't just think of upholstered seating. Instead, try quick-change covers for pillows, accent tables, or lampshades; even "bag" the chandelier with muslin, as they do in the South.

g A flirty pleated skirt is the perfect treatment for Clarence House's "Promenade Hindoue," an amusing Indian-inspired stripe. We used the green panel for the face of the pleats, and the white panel for the interior. The small red and white stripes along the back, seat, and pleats match the front of the slipcover.

h We loved the loose, romantic quality of Galbraith & Paul's "Sweet Pea" linen vine print. To capture that mood in a slipcover, we added a midcalf skirt, gathered only at the corners, and trimmed it with a 4-inch band of blue cotton canvas. The same blue cotton outlines the seat.

Because of the way a single stripe is centered from piece to piece, a chair in the corner becomes the visual focal point of a living room. Although the floor is bare wood, every piece of furniture, from the sofa to the ottomans, is softened with fabrics.

Opposite: A pair of delicately wrought French Regency–inspired chairs become surprising and inviting objects when covered in a dashing striped fabric that shows off their parts. A matching Roman shade is comprised of narrower stripes that help emphasize height in an otherwise low-ceilinged room.

Above: A diminutive love seat is fitted with a classic cool blue-and-white striped slipcover trimmed with a solid welting. The casual summery pattern is dressed up with a colorful throw pillow. The Roman shade features a classical scene framed by black borders.

Above: A lovely red-and-green floral vine appears to grow naturally, without interruption, from the top of the chair on to the seat, eventually reaching the freestanding footstool. Self-welting is used on both pieces of furniture.

Opposite: Nailheads need not be arranged in familiar linear patterns. Here, they are applied in a scrolling scalloped pattern at the bottom of the chair. The elegant curves of the wings are emphasized by nailheads that meet the armrests.

Opposite: Stripes are perfectly matched down
the fronts and sides of a pair of armless
chairs. Dining chairs are covered in solids and
detailed with a white welting that highlights
their distinctive shapes. Each of the shades on
an exuberantly scaled chandelier is covered in
a gold and yellow fabric.

Above: What appears simple is complex.
A single, center-placed stripe on the chair
harkens to horizontal bands on the curtains,
and others that run along the carpet. Another
striped pattern is revealed beneath the chair
pleat. The chair's blue-and-white welting tie
in with the curtains.

Above: *Simply Swedish. A pair of wooden chairs is slipcovered in a fresh white material that incorporates a narrow and vibrant red welting; heart motifs replicate the forms of the chair backs. Slipcovers are secured with cheerful and conspicuous red ties.*

Opposite: *Not unlike the lounge of a deluxe Art Moderne cruise ship, this room speaks of solidity and elegance. The restrained lines of the armchairs, sofa, and curtains are offset by bold horizontal stripes that course a pair of armless chairs.*

Opposite, above: *Leopards and tigers have left their marks in this luxurious room. Indeed, the high-ceilinged space is a virtual hunting ground for the eye as it captures the various faux animal prints, the stripes on the deep, angled armchairs, and the intricate geometric pattern on the curtains.*

Opposite, below: *Florals and stripes are combined on an inviting armchair and a delicate wooden chair notable for its beaded webbing arm supports. An exuberant candy-striping welting is used on the back and lower cushion of the armchair.*

Above: *This cozy sofa is dressed in casual, loose slipcover embellished with a self-welt. The footstool is crisply covered in a similar check with red trim separating the cap from the base. The grid of art on the wall echoes the check patterns used throughout the room.*

Opposite: *In keeping with this room's contemporary look, a pillow-back love seat is armless on one side while the other features a striking cylindrical support. Sitters in opposite-facing chairs have ready access to a padded, fabric-covered coffee table that can double as a bench.*

Above: *Broad brushstrokes of solid-colored fabrics result in a warm and dignified interior that easily accommodates a busily patterned floral floor runner, a multi-striped blanket, and a scroll-shaped pillow. Striped curtains are cut full and meet the floor with no break.*

Opposite, above: *The littlest item, a miniature chair covered in a faux leopard print, is the center of attention in a room that evokes elegant tropical splendor. A chaise longue is railroaded with narrow-band stripes, its texture made more conspicuous by deep button indentations.*

Opposite, below: *Getting the slip. An entire living room of furniture, including a small serving table, is made over with slipcovers in a cheerful pink-and-white check, all of which are trimmed in solid red welting. Dramatic curtain swags become decorative objects in themselves.*

Above: *This green-themed room evokes the outdoors but remains protected from it. Floral wallcoverings repeat on a chair (foreground, right), footstool, and swag of material concealing the contents of a copper storage bin. Earth-toned Roman shades mute the sun when necessary.*

117

CHAIRS

Opposite: *Plain, wide-planked floors are a perfect backdrop for fabrics. This allover airy floral textile didn't require complex engineering. A simple self-welting offers just the right edging.*

Above: *Casual, loose-fitting striped slipcovers, secured to chair seats, backs, and armrests with long dangling ties, are appropriate treatments, even for a formal dining room. Tablecloths, too, can be excessive, draping extravagantly on the floor.*

Above: *For a cozy guest bedroom, furnishings are subtly linked. A corner chair, covered in a tiny red-and-white check, features welting made of the same fabric that appears on the curtains, headboard, and tasseled bed skirt. The bottom of the chair is finished with a contrasting trim. White walls and bed linens prevent the floral theme from overwhelming the room.*

Opposite: *Climb aboard might be the operative phrase for a children's bed situated in an inviting, sculpted nook. The leopard-print chair features a bright pink welting that creates a strong contrast while echoing similar hues found on the throw pillows and quilt.*

ottomans & benches

Ottomans and benches are the items of furniture meant to fill leftover spaces in a room. And, yet, ottomans and benches often become the most inviting perches. Ottomans, at once decorative and practical, can be moved throughout a room at will. Benches, while solid and rigorous in form, have multiple functions and can take their place in any room of a house.

An ottoman large enough to become an alternative living room sofa is tufted into four pielike segments and finished at the bottom with fanciful fringe. The stripes are positioned to meet in the center, making for a piece of furniture that is supremely elegant but imbued with playfulness.

ottomans

Any piece of furniture able to serve more than one purpose in the home is a good thing. Even if space is not a consideration, an overscale ottoman more than pays its way as additional seating for a gathering, a resting place for stocking feet on movie night, a coffee table when overlaid with a tray, or with a functional hatch as a storage place for children's toys or extra bedding.

Our Ralph Lauren Fairfax square ottoman, upholstered on a wooden plinth base with turned bun feet, can accomplish all but the storage goal, but there are many on the market which also could have been chosen for that purpose. The challenge in upholstering a big piece is how to make it interesting—the design of the textile dictates the finished product, and the repeat of the pattern has to have the right rhythm over the frame. We upholstered our ottoman in the ultimate neutrals: black and white. Their strong contrasts add a fresh, chic look to any interior. Our use of everything from toiles to embossed leather, cut velvet to plaid, and stripes to witty line drawings illustrates how the fabric and finishes can set the mood in many different ways.

Henredon's graciously proportioned 40-inch-round ottoman contrasts with the rectilinear shape of the Ralph Lauren ottoman. While it may serve the same end, our decision to dress it up in velvet makes it seem a less appropriate place for feet, or for use as storage.

a

a "Peking Toile de Jouy" by Rose Cumming sets the tone for a chinoiserie boudoir or an elegant living room with casual Asian accents. The welted cap gives the ottoman a two-layered effect, but the pattern matches perfectly from the sides to the top.

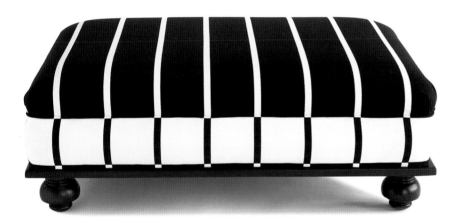

b

b The ottoman's continuous planes show off the fabric wonderfully. A strong example of a modern finished ottoman is Randolph & Hein's "Teso," whose bold piano-key stripes are set in opposition to each other in two contrasting colorways, on border and cap. The welting is cut straight instead of the more customary bias treatment, adding a crisp finishing touch.

c Clarence House's "Couvert de Feuilles," a cut velvet, was upholstered without interruption between the top and sides of the piece so as to give full rein to its organic, vine-like pattern. A coordinated black gimp circles the base.

c

decorator's tips

- An ottoman is wonderfully versatile: it's great for extra seating and can double as a coffee table if you place a tray on top of it.

- Velvets are woven from many fibers, including wool (mohair), cotton, silk, and synthetic blends. Each one has a different hand and durability.

- Patterns are created by techniques in weaving, cutting, crushing, and embossing (sometimes called gauffrage).

- A velvet's pile causes a "direction" in the fabric, which makes the fabric color appear to change when viewed from different angles. To avoid a two-tone effect, consider direction when you are upholstering a piece.

- Velvets are expensive, so treat them with care. Dry-clean only, and never iron.

DETAILS

Here we upholstered the ottoman with a separate side border and a welted and capped top, using Hinson & Co.'s "Calhoun Plaid." The welted cap gives the ottoman a two-layered effect. The welting was cut on the bias for a candy-striped look.

When working with stripes or plaids, a perfect match is crucial.

The addition of four black buttons on the cap and a row of nailheads at the edge of the wooden frame turn this ottoman into a perfect piece for a gentleman's study.

a

b

a "Beaufort Bonaparte" from Nobilis in rich garnet red, is an embossed velvet with a damask pattern pressed into the material after production by a burnished roller, using heat to maintain the design. This is an old technique, and a plethora of patterns already exist, so new colors and patterns—particularly as beautifully executed as this—will surely be noticed. Slightly tufted, and skirted with double panels to show the scale of the repeat, this ottoman might be well suited for the now-famous library designed by Albert Hadley for Mrs. Astor.

b "Orsay" from Pierre Frey is a standard linen velvet with a twist of Caribbean blue coloration, rich and saturated. Fully tufted, with fabric-covered buttons, we chose to nail-

head the scalloped edge at the top of the pleated skirt and to echo that scallop at the bottom of the skirt's panels. These simple variations successfully showcase the fabric and highlight the ottoman's curvy shape.

c "Benavides" from Bergamo is another color-saturated fabric, cut by means of an unusual technique that produces a unique textile. The rich green pattern displays linear cuts that outline leaf and petal forms. Untufted on the top surface, with a simple skirt, straight hem, and single welt of bias cut, we gave the color, pattern, ingenuity, and sheer beauty of this fabric the primary place.

d Finally, "Moreana" from Ardecora shows us the combination of a woven base-pile fabric inter-

spersed with a loose velvet print of large floral and leaf repeats. This weaving technique—in which a velvet pattern in a range of densities is woven intermittently on a plain ground fabric—is called brocaded velvet. Thought to have originated in China or Japan, brocaded velvet often employed lush silk threads as well as threads produced from silver or gold. Our slightly more modest but still opulent fabric displays a subtly nuanced color change between the espresso brown field and the brown-black velvet that appears on its surface. Our treatment left the top surface flat, so as to showcase most effectively the repeat and highlight the print; we then finished by reapplying brass nailheads and cutting a simple tailored skirt.

c

d

modern gustavian bench

This is a classic Swedish furniture piece—as utilitarian as it is handsome. Named for King Gustav III, who reigned from 1771 to 1792, the Gustavian style was a Swedish interpretation of the European antiques and decorative arts the king saw during his travels on the Continent. Using less expensive local woods and materials, the Swedish paid homage to fine European furnishings while developing a humbler, more pared down style of their own.

With its quintessentially simple shapes, symmetry, and painted woods, Swedish furniture is an excellent and viable option either as a specific decorating style or as part of an eclectic one. The palette of traditional Swedish fabrics consists usually of just two colors: white and another hue. Our bench has simple yet classically carved legs, a readed plinth, and unadorned, upholstered matching head and footboard; the latter is capped with a graceful curve and topped on its four corners with carved square rosettes and finials.

Upholstered in a range of fabrics, our example, Country Swedish's Gustavian Bench, could be at home almost anywhere. One issue worth bearing in mind is that of painted furniture and its physical presence, or "weight." The bench is painted gray-white, so when selecting the fabric to be upholstered onto the frame it is necessary to consider the weight of the finished piece. Fabrics with white or neutral tones will act to "lighten" the bench, allowing it to blend into the room. This lightening can be furthered by matching the secondary color in the fabric throughout the room. This dual-chromatic approach, especially when applied to the sparse aesthetic of Swedish interiors, can appear opulent as well as quite soothing by virtue of the simple palette and repetition of color. Of course, the contrary approach yields a different result altogether: Contrasting a brightly colored and perhaps unexpected color field in a fabric lends weight and substance to the bench.

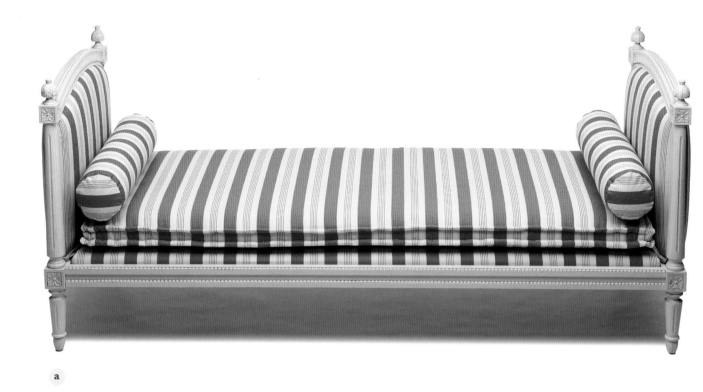

a

b

DETAILS

Perhaps the most subtle and delicate of our choices is the "Bagnols Cotton Print," a Brunschwig & Fils fabric. Its palette of red and white follows the Swedish tradition of using just two colors, although it is nearly completely white, scattered with an irregular stripe of rectangles, and interspersed with plainly drawn floral sprigs.

The use of bias-cut single welts on the bolster ends and cushion edges further simplifies the style, and we used a soft pink-red gimp to edge the upholstery as well as to edge the bolster cushions. Although the gimp is only an inch wide, it lends an air of sophistication and finish to this demure fabric.

Extremely subtle, small, fabric-covered buttons are scattered in a diamond pattern on the seat mattress; they are not visible at first glance but make a perfect final touch to marry this delicate fabric to the striking carved frame.

a b Among our choices, "Sail Broad Stripe" from Jane Churchill (a), and "Gripsholm Check" from Country Swedish (b), are the most faithful to the traditional two-color palette of Gustavian style. These fabrics are humble yet elegant, cautiously and rhythmically placed and upholstered onto our bench. On the stripe detailing is kept simple, with no welting on the bolsters. A classic mattress stitch finishes the loose cushion edge both top and bottom (allowing the cushion to flip in the event of spillage). The same mattress edge finish was utilized on the check fabric, but a little more liberty was taken with upholstery detail. Dressmaker's flourishes show up on the gathered ends of the bolsters with matching fabric-covered buttons to punctuate their ends, as well as to create six indentations into the mattress seat.

c

d

e

c Lee Jofa's "Trianon Toile" works perfectly with the bench by virtue of both its coloration and the architectural nature of its pattern. The large surface of the mattress cushion as well as the outside arm panels are perfect uninterrupted planes upon which to consider the intricate characters and buildings incorporated into this design. The ratio of background white to printed coral/brick red is almost equal, and so a balance is struck, making this a piece which neither hides itself in the wings, nor hogs the spotlight. Readily available cords, attached to tape for ease of sewing into edges, have been added here on both the bolsters and the seat cushion as a pleasing detail. The real challenge here is for the upholstery to match flawlessly across the edge of the mattress to its border, as the building images punctuate each corner.

d The last of the fabrics with a light ground—"Crewel Embroidery" from Lee Behren Silks—also appears to strike a balance between the colored trellis, leaf, and floral pattern and the white ground. This pattern is bold, medium in scale, and requires no welting to interrupt the careful cutting and pattern-matching.

e In contrast, the two fabrics with dark grounds and white prints clearly illustrate the difference between the airy and windswept Brunschwig cotton (see Details box) and the greater weight added on by the use the bolder color. "Graham" from Kathryn Ireland, with its hand-carved woodblock motif interspersed with crosses and jewels, is a clear and fresh departure from the standard for this frame.

f

g

h

f "Cupola," from Anna French, has a loose and youthful feel with its concentric circles of small white dots. Since the field color is so strong, we picked up the color of the frame by welting the cushion and bolsters with a fresh white linen. To continue in that vein, the upholstered sections of the frame were also piped in a double row of white linen.

g **h** Modern and totally unexpected, both "Lulu" from Angela Adams (g) and "Evil Eye" from Lulu DK Fabrics (h), offer a range of decorative possibilities. For "Evil Eye," we cut off the small paisley border and used it to edge the plinth of the bench and as a trim around the bolster edges.

decorator's tips

- To be faithful to the style of a classic Swedish bench, choose fabrics in two tones but have fun experimenting with a variety of designs.

- Fabrics with dark grounds give more weight to a piece.

- Fabrics with selvage borders, like Lulu DK Fabrics' "Evil Eye" (h), offer many decorative possibilities. We cut off the small paisley border and used it to edge the plinth of the bench and as a trim around the bolsters.

- Before button-tufting a fabric with a stripe in the design, like Brunschwig & Fils' Bagnols print, (see Details box) lay it out on the piece and decide how many tufts you want and how they should be distributed.

- Geometric patterns require the most careful matching.

trestle bench

Like an ottoman, a trestle bench can take on many different roles—extra seating, coffee table, or footrest. In an entry hall it's useful for removing shoes or preparing for an outing. In a bedroom it could hold books or clothes at the foot of the bed. Thomas O'Brien's Trestle Bench, inspired by an 1880s English bench with a leather seat, is a versatile piece that can live happily in town or in the country.

a

b

c

d

a b c d

This upholstery lesson is all about lines and how to arrange them. Think about the width and scale of the stripes in each fabric, then play with the verticals and horizontals. We experimented with running wide stripes from end to end, which would widen a narrow bedroom if the bench were placed at the foot of the bed. With "Hamaca Azul" from Donghia (a), we railroaded the stripes on the seating area. At the same time, we cut across the warp to join the meticulously matched pieces together to form the border adjoining the wood. Here, an interesting use of nailheads, symmetrically spaced and used in a double row vertically, show the versatility that can be achieved with a little creative planning.

Some fabrics looked best upholstered perpendicular to the frame. Les Toiles du Soleil's "Collioure," (b) a wide-warped fabric with an asymmetrical repeat pattern of wide and narrow stripes, works as a perfect contrast to the stately rhythm of the ridged and symmetrical bench frame. The overscaled silver-tone pyramid nailheads that punctuate the line between wood and fabric add a fanciful note. "Rio" from Manuel Canovas (c), is cut with the stripes running front to back of the bench; the border that joins the top to the frame is cut to form a single color.

The use of nailheads as a finishing detail at the wood's edge takes its historical cue from the days before decorative cord, gimp, and tassels were used on upholstery. The nailhead is actually a cousin of the original tack, once considered (with cautious spacing) an acceptable finish detail on upholstery. Indeed, examples of tack-finished furniture can be seen right up to the twentieth century in historical settings and furniture museums.

The decorative nailhead, once a humble circle of finished metal on the end of a nail, has undergone a metamorphosis: Faux-leather, gilded gold stars, and polished chrome diamond nailheads, to name just a few, can now be found at reputable upholstery supply shops although the more esoteric examples are best obtained through designers and architects.

As is often seen in English upholstery finishes, nailheads are frequently used together with decorative tapes, trims, and gimps, spaced strategically to showcase both the trim and the nailhead. We see an example of such an application on "Challis Stripe II" from Old World Weavers (d). A flat tape was cut from the pale section of the fabric's woven stripe, and—working from the center out and using a template for spacing—black nailheads were carefully placed to achieve a dual trimmed effect.

Opposite: *Like a blue velvet cloud that has drifted through the multi-paned, sky-sized window, an elegantly tailored ottoman invites repose. Its brown trim, narrow at the top, broader at the base, harkens to the wood of the floor and chairs. Strategically placed yellow pillows brighten the room.*

This oversize ottoman set on turned bun feet
doubles as a coffee table when a serving tray is
placed upon it. Buttons create deep tufts, while
the corners are emphasized with neat pleats.
The pattern repeats on a matching throw pillow.

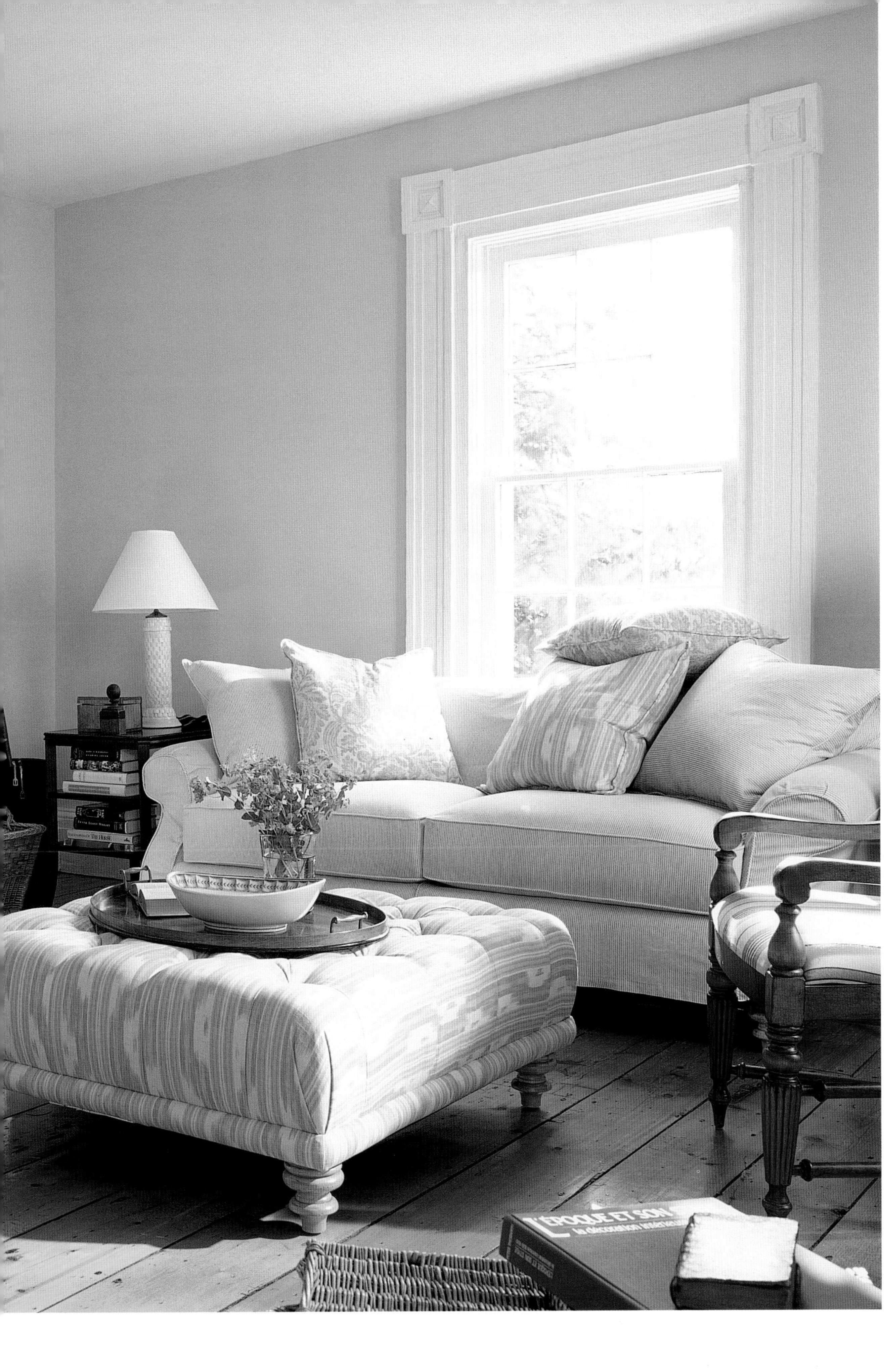
L'ÉPOQUE ET SON

Opposite: *Green velvet is used to define an ottoman/coffee table as the centerpiece in a regal living room. Corners are pleated to reveal a contrasting fabric. Self-welting is knotted at each corner.*

Above: *Zebra stripes on an ottoman seamlessly leave their mark from the top to the bottom of the plinth. Black welting fosters a layered effect. Nailheads define the lower border. Elsewhere in the room, pillows and a chair back are treated with varying sizes of checks.*

Shades and curtains both conceal the world that lies outside the walls as well as announce it. Whether it's a simple Roman shade that can be rolled up or down, a blind that can let in a little or a lot of light, or luxurious curtains fitted with a valance and decorative hardware, what we use to cover a window becomes one of the most important interior details.

window treatments

At whatever point these Roman shades are rolled down, they become solid blocks of color that harmonize with the room's furnishings and decorative details, including the bold striped footstools with their matching oversized cushions.

roman shades

A window shade controls the light, passage of air, and amount of privacy in a room. It also defines the decoration of a window. Whether made of a textile or another material (wood, parchment, or some other), a window shade opens and closes vertically instead of horizontally like standard curtains. Fabric shades have been in and out of vogue too often to mention, but there is little doubt they offer the largest number of options for a window treatment while using the least amount of fabric. This presupposes making a Roman shade, or a variation thereof, where a flat piece of fabric constitutes the body of the shade (plus any linings). The standard rule of thumb for measuring fabric is 30 inches in addition to the length of the shades, and—if the window is wider than the fabric—two equal lengths. As for a bedspread, it is unusual to place a seam in the center, so a window 96 inches wide would use one full panel of fabric in the center, with two pieces (cutting the second length in half vertically and sewing it to the sides of the center) seamed on the side.

All the shades here are a variation of the simple flat Roman model, and quite easy to construct. If linings and interlinings as well as decorative trims are desired, it may be best to seek out the assistance of a professional, since these details make construction more complicated.

First, decide if the shade will be mounted with IB (Inside Bracket, a trade term referring to the inside casing of the windows, framed by any decorative moldings) or OB (Outside Bracket, referring to the mounting, often several inches above and outside the moldings and the window frame). There are many reasons to choose one over the other. IB shades allow the frame to show, can display a trim paint color, and are more confined and simple. IB is also almost always the right choice if a second window treatment (such as curtains) will be hung on the window. In such a case, the Roman shade might be unlined and simply made to diffuse light and afford privacy, while the curtains may have a lining designed to darken the room for sleeping.

OB shades are usually chosen if there is an unattractive window surround, and if no curtains will be used. They can be manufactured with "returns": fabric flaps that cover the board on which the shade is mounted to the wall, so that seen in profile, the mechanism for raising and lowering the shade is not visible.

If you are uncertain which style to adopt, look through several decorating magazines, and mark any designs that you find particularly interesting. The cost of a shade is determined by several factors. First is the fabric itself, and its stated price. Second is the style of shade: gathered shades (also referred to as balloon shades) can take as many yards to make as a pair of curtains, so be judicious about your design idea. If you must have the fuller style, choosing a simpler and less expensive fabric, and perhaps adding a trim for extra pizzazz, can save you money. Shop around: many small fabric retailers manufacture shades. Ask to see examples of their work (samples are usually hanging in a showroom) and look carefully at the craftsmanship. Keep in mind that a shade hangs, raises, and lowers by the use of lift cords. These are threaded through a series of small rings sewn to the reverse side of the shade in intervals determined by the design of the shade, as well as by the pattern of the fabric.

Finally, the placement of the bottom row of rings will determine if there is a "skirt" or final flap of fabric exposed as the shade goes up and down. This is most important when a trim (beads, ribbons, fringes, and the like) has been attached to the bottom of the shade. If the trim is to be seen, careful placement of the first horizontal row of rings (when fastened to the end of the lift cords) is essential.

While all our nine examples are flat Roman shades, they show three different ways of using the lift cords and offer three distinct options for the finished look. The Rogers & Goffigon (a), Luciano Marcato (b), and Thompson (c) fabrics, as well as the horizontally striped "Melker" from Sandberg (d), are all constructed with a straight hem to raise and lower uniformly. In the same category but with a dressmaker's twist, Clarence House's "Vortice" (e), with its scalloped bottom and wooden beads, is constructed the same way but shows one of the many variations one can employ by cutting the hemline irregularly.

The second design is shown in the shades made from fabrics by Schumacher (f) and Scalamandré (g), and from Lulu DK Fabrics' "Moondance" (h), in which the lift cords are set in from the outer edge of the shade to allow its edges to drop. (This is sometimes referred to as a "drop tail shade.") This treatment can be used either IB or OB, but lends itself to the latter, as its softened edges (created by the drooping outer lines) work well to camouflage an unsightly casement.

a The Rogers & Goffigon shade is made with two colors of glazed linen, called "Somerset", seamed together, red on top of white. Its graphic design required an extremely careful face design as well as ring placement in order to maximize the design's effect and have the wave patterns repeat upon the raising of the shade.

b Great care had to be taken with Luciano Marcato's "Soli e Lune," since the fabric is thin and the shade was left unlined to allow the light to shine through. Rows of half-inch, blue-striped grosgrain ribbon are stitched up and down the shade's face, so that a reinforced section of fabric would allow the attachment of rings on the reverse side.

c

d

c Because silk is fragile and fades easily, this fabric, Jim Thompson's "Ranong," was lined and interlined. For a graphic accent, a 2½-inch fabric tape with a Greek key design was added. It was inset ¾-inch along the sides and bottom edge. In order to have the Greek keys line up, the center panel was made slightly wider than the sides.

d This big stripe pattern, "Melker" from Sandberg, was run horizontally but reengineered so that all the colors in the repeat would appear in the folds when the shade was pulled up. The pink stripe was seamed at the top and we made sure the brown stripe fell at the bottom to give the shade visual weight. The shade also has a blackout lining, which adds body and helps the stripes hang straight.

e To echo the swirls in this design, "Vortice" by Clarence House, the bottom edge of the shade was scalloped and adorned with a wooden-bead trim. Because the fabric's ground is white, a flat black half-inch welt was added to define the top.

f "Rajasthan Paisley," a cotton paisley from Schumacher, was lined to give it a bit more structure. To complement the exotic motif, half-inch green satin ribbon was stitched to the bottom edge and adorned with glamorous beaded trim. The weight of the beads gives the hem a slight scallop when the shade is raised.

g

h

g Scalamandré's "Palmier" is a traditional English design. This shade was lined and interlined, and tassels and glass beads were added for extra embellishment. For both, the first row of rings has been sewn in place to allow the trim to show when the shade is in operation.

h "Moondance" from Lulu DK Fabrics has borders on each selvage, but the window was too narrow for both borders to show. We cut them off and restitched them to the shade like tapes on a Venetian blind. The shade's bottom has drop-tail edges that fall gracefully on each side when the shade is raised.

i   Sahco Hesslein's "Pictura" has been made as an unconstructed Roman shade. Here only two lift cords are used on the outer edges, and four extra pleats have been added at the bottom—these allow for a simple and ultimately graceful scallop as the lowered shade is raised. One oval is centered at the top of the shade so that the repeat formed a diamond pattern.

decorator's tips

- Before you create the design of your Roman shade, think about what function it will perform.

- Sunlight adversely affects many fabrics. Before selecting a material for a shade, note which direction the window faces. Line and interline delicate fabrics, or place them only in windows that aren't exposed to direct sunlight.

- Consider what your shade will look like both up and down. Designs can be adjusted and folds embellished to make the shade look attractive in both positions.

- For an affordable couture look, use inexpensive solid fabrics for the shade itself and splurge on luxurious trim.

- You won't have to add trim fabric at all if you use shade fabrics with borders, which can stand alone as edging or be cut and reapplied as hems, stripes, or valances.

curtains

Curtains (or the equally correct but spurned term *draperies*) are meant to serve a purpose. Perhaps they appeared first as bed hangings rather than as window treatments, to be closed for privacy and keep in warmth. With curtains, form definitely follows function. Deciding what the curtains will be used for precedes even the choice of fabric. Light adjustment, draft control, privacy, as well as ever-present aesthetic considerations, need to be clearly addressed if a window treatment is to be successful.

Layers, linings, and valances all play into this equation. Black chintz, for example, may be sewn as an interlining (fabric hanging between the face and the lining) to deflect sunlight. On the other hand, an unlined sheer print can afford privacy from outside, yet allow in a varying degree of ambient light. A valance can serve to hide a multitude of sins, notably the mechanical traverse rod designed to open and close curtains easily. In our example, a wooden ½-inch plywood board is cut and shaped to the desired finish, and fitted with returns (pieces of wood used as the sides) and a mounting board (the "lid" to the box from which the window treatment will be suspended).

One distinct advantage of a cornice—an upolstered valance—is that it displays the fabric on a flat surface, and affords an opportunity to show the sections of the most desirable "repeat" or pattern. Having curtains hang from underneath not only hides the opening mechanism, but allows the eye to see the fabric in both its flat and gathered states.

A simple rule of thumb for the amount of fabric required applies when considering a solid fabric. Multiply the width of the window by $2\frac{1}{2}$ and divide by the width of the material to get a rough idea of how many panels of fabric you need. The window door featured here measures 100" across, and thus needs 250" in width. If we divide the 250" by the width of the fabric to be used (most range from 48 to 60" with 54" being the standard), we can conclude that we need five lengths of material. This would result in a pair of curtains with two solid panels sewn together down the center, and a half width (a full length panel split vertically) sewn to the outer edges. The resulting 125" of fabric for each side of the window can then be lined as necessary and pleated to approximately 50 to 60", allowing for the curtains to open and close completely without looking overstretched.

When patterns are being considered as fabric choices, several additional considerations apply. Given the above example, if the finished length of the curtains is 90", and the repeat is 25", four repeats (or 100") of fabric are required per length of raw material. This is to ensure that the panels, when sewn together, have the same motif at the top of each panel. The additional 50" (or $1\frac{1}{2}$ yards) seem unnecessary, but this is the case, as the hems use the remaining 10" per cut.

The selection of printed fabric forces one to consider breaking with the rule of thumb. An over-scale pattern, or one with distinctive characters or markings, may require

a

b

c

d

e

f

g

h

WINDOW TREATMENTS

less fabric. For example, "Palma" from Manuel Canovas (h), with its large and whispy fern pattern, would be lost in a jumble of fabric if gathered at a ratio of 2.5 to 1. Here, a modest 1.5 to 1 allows for the pattern to show gracefully and still imparts the luxury of the fabric. This is a situation where a flannel interlining (hanging between the face and lining fabrics) can add substance and weight to otherwise limp curtains. This is one of the ways to compensate for the changes in yardage.

The question of surface embellishment should also be considered. While large and baroque trims might have been standard in the grand rooms of Europe's palaces, today's nine-foot ceiling is a luxury, so simple is better. This in no way

implies a lack of design creativity, as a staggering array of raw materials have been turned into a seemingly endless number of trims, available from craft stores and shops that specialize in passementerie. Woven braids, ribbons in a multitude of colors and prints, beads of glass, wood, and polymers; natural ropes and fringes of raffia, hand-tied tassels of silk, and combinations of all of these are readily purchased. Choosing the right embellishment can be tricky, and often the trained eye of a professional who understands the parameters of the room's overall design is helpful.

Green-and-white grosgrain ribbon adds snap to Marimekko's "Kevatlita Lime" (c), while Carleton V's "Printemps" (d) is set off with simple white cording. "Big

Apple Stripe" from Dek Tillet (b) and "Nicobar Camaieu" from Pierre Frey (g) were so graphic on their own, no embellishment was needed. Calico Corner's "Limerick" check (a) was cut on the full bias to make a diamond-pattern border—a classic dressmaker detail.

Natural trims work well with the green hues seen in these fabrics. Kathryn Ireland's "Ikat Check" (f) looks fetching with raffia fringe. Manuel Canovas' "Palma" (h) and Greeff's "Zipper" stripe (e) were decked out with wooden beads.

A good rule of thumb: less is more. We are less likely to tire of a simple fabric-covered cord than a multicolored fringe. The secret is in understanding the function of the curtain and the amount of emphasis desired in the window dressing.

curtains hung on rings

Without a valance, precise measuring is of utmost importance and is often done after hanging to ensure the desired length. When trims are applied, further care is required with regard to their placement over the pattern, and the combination of materials must be checked for suitability. The formula already discussed for calculating fabric quantity applies here, too. Fabric should be cut with consideration for the pattern, and a 20% floor-to-ceiling ratio used as a starting point for the length of the valance, if there is one.

a

b

c

d

e

f

g

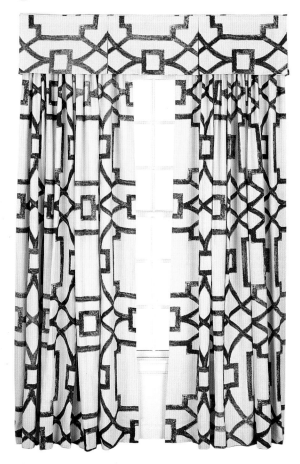

h

decorator's tips

- We worked with three types of fabric patterns: tight repeats, large-scale repeats, and solids. For large-scale repeats, one should use less fullness across the window so that the design can be seen. Panels made from smaller patterns and solids can have more width.

- The usual rule for the ratio of valance to curtain length is 1 to 5. Use your eye and the fabric design to adjust this formula.

- Light control, climate control, and sturdiness are all good reasons for lining curtains. But if you desire to have a billowing effect or filtered daylight, skip this step.

- For a traditional hemline, panels should break 1½ inches on the floor; for a "puddle" effect, allow for 3 inches on the floor. Clean, modern-style panels should just skim the floor. Do-it-yourselfers should measure hems on the rod.

To give these window treatments a modern appeal, we chose graphic fabrics, hung as simple panels either from dark-stained wooden rings on a matching pole or with soft valances. Minimal trimmings were used.

a We created a wide-wave stripe by using Kvadrat's "Divina" in two contrasting solids. The fabric was cut with pinking shears and rejoined in horizontal bands. The curtain tops have no pleats; they were attached to the rings at 8-inch intervals. This is a substantial wool and did not have to be lined.

b For this Zoffany blend, we used a standard 3-prong pinch pleat for the panels, inserted 4 inches from the top. We placed the pleating in the middle of each stripe to emphasize the color contrast and verticality.

c Dark-brown bands outline and ground this modern floral print,

Alan Campbell's "Potalla." The top band is 1½-inch wide and the bottom is 6 inches. The panel tops have 1½-inch pinch pleats that are caught at the top by the wooden rings. Cable tiebacks blend into the fabric's ground.

d These traditional curtains bow to the English country-house look. Made out of Brunschwig & Fils' "Birds of a Feather," they are interlined with flannel, pencil-pleated at the top, and have an attached 18-inch valance trimmed with multicolored fringe.

e These silk curtains, fashioned from Silk Trading Company's "Taffeta Solid" and "Kopla Silk," were bordered with a 3-inch band of copper silk on the inner edge and along the hemline. Tiny tuck pleats at the tops of the panels give luxurious billows to the unlined fabric.

f Here we used an inverted box pleat on each panel (Designers Guild's "Corazon"), which places most of the gathering and fullness on the back side of the curtain and works well with large repeats and modern patterns.

g The wavy movement in the fabric's pattern, "Ananas" by Raoul Textiles, was the perfect line to follow in the valance, which is trimmed with a self cording to accentuate the scallop shape. The panels are untrimmed to allow the print to speak for itself.

h To make the 3-panel box-pleated soft valance, we cut and matched the fretwork pattern ("Fretwork-Wainscot" by Michael Devine) so that the design would fall symmetrically. Careful planning was also needed to make sure the pattern matched properly at the inner edge of each panel.

Above: A dramatically scaled floor-to-ceiling corner window is announced and enhanced by a sweeping expanse of draperies set on unadorned rods. Throughout the room, fabric is a major decorative element, making a statement as slipcovers, as a floral print, and in velvet. A backless sofa provides sitters with unobscured views indoors and out.

Opposite: In a sunny bathroom, a pair of windows is fitted with Chinese-motif Roman shades that provide necessary privacy, yet are sheer enough to preserve some light. Wall tiles, sconce shades, soap dishes, and window treatments color coordinate.

Opposite, above: *Window treatments and furniture fabrics match in a folksy bedroom. Valances are fashioned with decorative curves and trimmed with a design of white flowers, also used to trim the gathered shades.*

Opposite, below: *A nearly floor-to-ceiling folding screen proves an ideal surface for showing off a large repeat pattern that also appears on the valance and curtains. The valance and curtains are trimmed with a blue-and-white fringe.*

Above: *An otherwise open plan dining area/kitchen is easily made into separate rooms by suspending two panels of all-white unlined curtains on shower rings. A clean, modern look is achieved by ensuring that the panels meet the floor precisely with no breaking of material.*

Above: A detail from a large-scale repeating botanical pattern is centered on the valance; the pattern appears again on throw pillows set on an earth-toned sofa outlined in crisp white welting. With curtains that incorporate so many colors, virtually every object and furnishing in this library becomes an appropriate match.

Opposite: Billowing red-and-white striped curtains appear always to be filled with a breeze, an effect that imbues the room with a fresh sense of the outdoors. The casual drape of the curtains is tempered by a subtle, yet formal, trim at the bottom.

small touches

The details of a room often become the main statements. Furnishings thought of as ancillary to a room's décor—upholstered headboards, portable folding screens, tablecloths, storage units—work to unify a larger design statement while sometimes becoming the most conspicuous interior detail. These are items we need in a house and they are worth making as beautiful as possible.

The visual focal points of this clean-lined, serene bedroom are the matching rectangular headboard and skirt. Apart from the footstool and rug, the stripes are the room's only patterned surfaces; their hues set the tone for the rest of the décor.

folding screens

Folding screens offer many opportunities in home decoration. With limitless shapes, widths, and heights (not to mention surface decorations), a folding screen can cover a multitude of sins. The perfect solution as a portable wall, room partition, headboard, dressing area, decorative accent, or as a means to hide a big-screen TV, folding screens have long been a favorite of interior designers. Usually easy to make (depending on size and embellishments), a do-it-yourselfer could easily construct this useful accessory. A furniture-grade plywood frame, some burlap or muslin to reinforce the interior, and a fabric to cover the screen is all one needs.

Guidelines for consideration are some of the following: a proportionate floor to ceiling height (12 to 18" below the ceiling is usual), shape and profile, fabric, and detail. Small repeats, wovens, and solids can provide the opportunity for surface decoration. Ribbons, buttons, cords, braids, and nail heads are most frequently used, but notions shops can provide an endless number of details to enliven simple textiles. When designing the screen, remember that they can do double duty: a vivid print on one side reversing to a coordinating stripe on the back gives you the summer "slipcover" version of a second look.

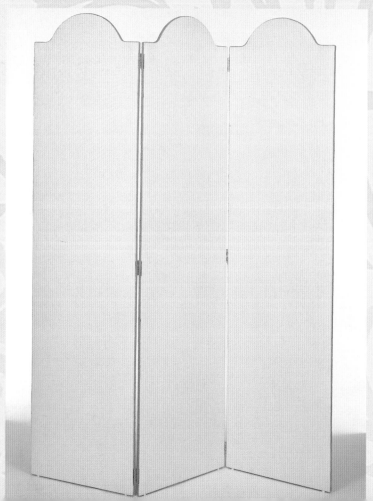

a The architectural pattern of "Labyrinth" from Lulu DK Fabrics required careful matching of the lines from panel to panel. The edges are trimmed with a jute binding.

b To frame this lavish paisley print, "Manoje" from Lorenzo Rubelli, we cut the border of the fabric and resewed it on the edge of the screen's two outside panels.

c Stripes add visual height to a room. Here, the fabric, "Chittagong Stripe" by Nina Campbell, was placed so that the dark brown stripe is the first color on the left side of each panel, which helps ground the strong pattern.

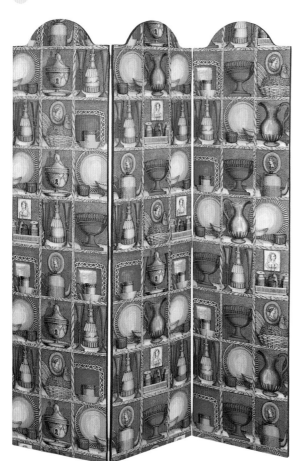

d Summer Hill Ltd.'s "Ribbon Cascade," a romantic ribbon print, forms a graceful lattice design on the screen. To keep the pattern flowing from panel to panel, we meticulously matched each section.

e To center the floral motif and allow the pink stripe to outline each panel and fit the frame, Clarence House's "Rayure Coromandel" was cut and resewn, eliminating some of the white ground.

f This trompe l'oeil print, Luciano Marcato's "Ventrina con Oggetti," was lined up so that a different piece of pottery is pictured on the top row of each panel.

g The weathered finish on Pierre Frey's charming "Petit Parc" gives it an antique look. The ribbons were aligned and one of the three motifs—basket, bird, and bouquet—were centered at the top of each panel. The edges were finished with navy blue gimp.

h The French calligraphy in golden script on Carolyn Quartermaine's "French Script" forms the repeat on this fabric. The title "La Description" was placed at the top center of each panel and the rest of the pattern was allowed to fall from there.

i The lyrical repeat of "Wheaton" from Travers was allowed to wander across each panel without regard to pattern matching. A simple jute braid outlines the edges.

headboards

The bed is the focal point of the bedroom, and an upholstered headboard makes a statement and offers limitless opportunities for design. Upholstered headboards, either simple and solid, or extravagant French button-tufted, have long been an important part of the well-dressed bedroom. They can be made in a wide variety of shapes and sizes, and the conventional marketplace overflows with options. Sturdy and supportive as a headrest when reading or as simple room decoration, upholstered headboards are fairly economical to make and can be easily reworked to change their look over time. With headboard slipcovers, a second look is easily achieved: once the pattern is cut using simple muslin, a quick change is possible whenever the urge strikes.

Headboards are available through many catalogs and home-furnishing shops, and they can be delivered and bolted to a standard metal bed frame in no time at all. An adventurous spirit might choose to design this item, since a well-thought-out design and a modicum of skill with a jigsaw and staple gun offer endless possibilities. Headboards are constructed in two standard ways—a consumer might choose a ready-made wooden surround (Swedish style) or a headboard completely covered in fabric. Stretching, gathering, buttoning, bordering, and piping are only a few of the ways to embellish the frame, and they provide an endless number of style opportunities.

If you do design your own headboard, give it very careful consideration, since it may also act as a room divider, a shelf, or a foil for a curtain-hung bed. Again, remember the cardinal rule: form follows function.

"Folies du Jardin" from Suzanne Bonser for Altizer (a), a pretty lavender toile, was upholstered on a three-panel headboard. The petite scale of Clarence House's "Herbier" (b), a sunny yellow toile, complements the arched headboard, which is trimmed with a double row of dressmaker's raffia in crisp white. "Carousel Stripe" from Jane Churchill (c) is used on the inset panel of a Swedish-style headboard. The panel, which takes just two yards of fabric, can be popped out and the fabric easily changed with the help of a staple gun. Robert Allen's "Highridge" chintz (d) in kiwi green dresses up an elegant, curvy headboard. Raoul Textiles' "Miranda" (e) is trimmed with a band of pale blue.

An ogee-shaped headboard upholstered in "Brandolini Fuchsia" from Travers (f) spices up any dull bedroom, as does the headboard upholstered in Holland & Sherry red wool felt (g) and embroidery floss tufts. Marimekko's "Kivet" (h) takes polka dots to the extreme, and last, Calico Corner's coral print (i) and headboard is a classic.

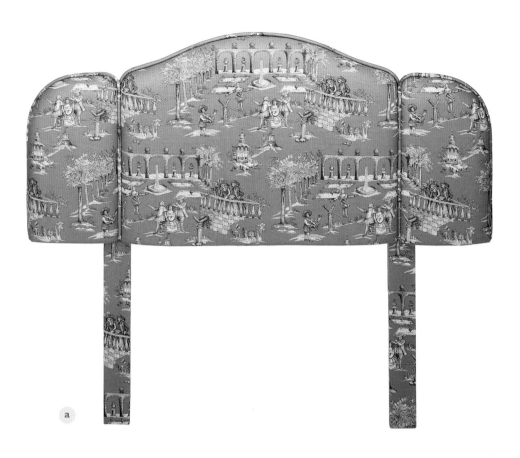

a

b

c

d

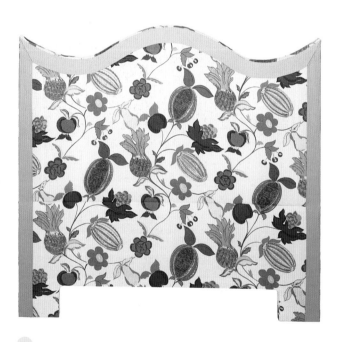

e

f

g

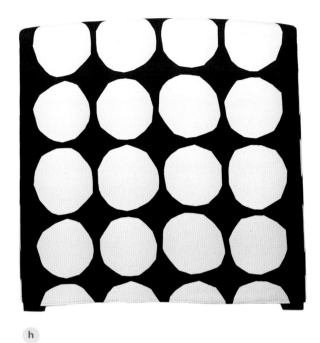

h

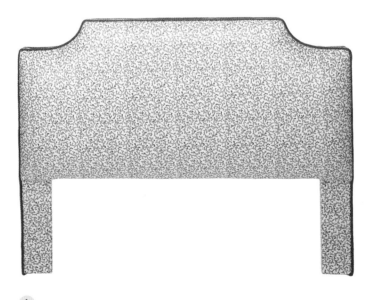

i

decorator's tips

- All headboards pictured are queen size and attach easily to a standard metal frame for a mattress and box spring.

- Today's mattress sets are often extra thick. Before ordering a custom headboard, measure the height from the floor to the top of your mattress so that your upholsterer can build it to the right proportions.

- If you think up an unusual headboard style, have your upholsterer make a template of the shape so you can be sure it works.

- Guest rooms are the place to take risks: bright colors make houseguests happy.

- If you redecorate frequently, add slipcovers to your headboards.

tablecloths

Much like the folding screen, a graciously appointed fabric-covered table can provide a decorating opportunity to solve a vast number of problems. The base table can be found through many sources and at many price levels, and the fabric can be anything from duck cloth to silk, depending on the budget. As the seasons pass, new cloths can either be purchased ready-made or sewn to provide a change of scenery, while the dry-cleaned original hangs in the closet waiting for its next day in the sun. Almost anyone with a bit of skill on a sewing machine can produce a smart and chic tablecloth by following a simple formula for yardage requirements and manufacturing technique.

When working out the yardage required, add the diameter in inches to twice the length of the skirt from top of table to floor. (Adding an inch to the latter gives a graceful break on the floor.) For example, if the table is 48" in diameter and 30" to the floor from the top surface, you will need a 108" tablecloth without a break on the floor, or 110" with a break. Dividing that number by the width of the chosen fabric provides you with the number of "lengths" required to sew together a wide enough cloth, as well as taking into account the length of the cut (the 108" cloth requires at least 114" to account for the hems and seams, assuming a 1" hem and seam allowance). Thus, with a 60"-wide piece of material, two lengths of 114" (or a total of 228" of material), are required.

As a rule, the fabric is not joined by a center seam. A solid band of material remains in the center, and the second length is cut in half and sewn to the two sides. This avoids having a seam in the center of the finished cloth. Folding the fabric in half first by the width, and again carefully by the length, provides an apex from which to pivot a ruler. Marking slowly with a tailor's chalk at three 4" intervals around the quarter circle, and cutting outside those marks for hemming, provides the cloth. (Repeating the process a second time with lining, and pinning them together, will give you a professionally lined cloth).

Surface embellishments can be varied and include welting (or cord), tape trim, tassels, fringe, or beads to name a few. The rule is that the table will rarely stand alone with its cloth, so less is often more when it comes to details. Once the lamp, books, candles, table settings, or flowers are in place, the over-the-top trim may seem just that. That said, a tablecloth is an easily changed item, so it is feasible to indulge in the outrageous on special occasions and have an alternative for everyday use.

Cleaning is an important consideration with tablecloths. Dry cleaning is the best bet for most cloths, but if you intend to wash the cloth (either commercially or at home), consider prewashing and drying the fabric several times before it is made up to ensure that all shrinkage and fading have occurred at the raw material stage. It is also wise to test a ½-yard piece of material for colorfastness before choosing a material that will need to be laundered. A brilliant red may become bubble-gum pink in the wash and not what you intended.

Overcloths (or squares of a second fabric) positioned over the floor-length cloth are another way to change the mood. A Wedgewood-blue cloth covered by a summery white print can bring a fresh breeze to a room while a contrasting orange print square would be a sophisticated accent to a cocktail party.

And don't forget about the storage space available under the cloth. When space is limited, you get the bonanza of another closet.

a

b

c

d

e

f

g

h

i

With a circular folding table—ours has a 48-inch diameter and seats six to eight people—and seven yards of fabric for a tablecloth, you can create instant ambience. Choose fabrics with bold colors or amusing patterns that will set the mood for an entertaining evening.

Bright stripes and checks are festive and play visual tricks on a round surface. Both "Admiral's Stripe" from Kirk Brummel (a) and Donghia's "Hamaca Rojo" multi-colored stripe (b) offer an opportunity either to manipulate the pattern or leave it alone. We cut and mitered "Admiral's Stripe" in concentric squares for a crisp regimental effect, and simply allowed the Donghia stripe to fall naturally over the circular table.

Jim Thompson's "Similan" silk check (c) reads as a check or a stripe, depending on how the iridescent pattern catches the light. Additional shimmer comes from tiny petal-shaped glass beads stitched to the skirt. "Bombay," a green linen floral paisley from Raoul Textiles (h), and Gaston y Daniela's large-scale botanical print (g) will whisk your guests off to a fanciful garden. "Sultan," by China Seas (e), conjures up stories of the Arabian nights by Scheherazade, while Andrew Martin's lyrical blue-and-white "Moncogran," with its embroidered crest pattern (f), is reminiscent of Camelot's knights of the round table. A sunny summer day is the mood of Lucretia Moroni's "Amercanda" sheer linen print overskirt (i), while Squigee's funky star burst (d) wittily brings outer space into even the most-down-to-earth home.

Trimming the hems of the skirts with lavish fringes or simple grosgrain and velvet ribbons adds the perfect finishing touch. Other practical touches to consider include using a felt liner the same size as the tablecloth to give a layer of body and softness underneath, and a 48-inch diameter round glass top to protect the glamorous cloth.

storage unit

These industrial metal shelves, transformed with fabrics into stylish movable closets, instantly solve the problem of where to store belongings in a small space. Perfect for a number of uses, available in a variety of sizes, a fabric-covered storage unit can even transform the mundane TV and stereo equipment stand into a design statement. Like a tablecloth, the storage rack slipcover is easily changeable and can be used seasonally. Fancier valances and mitered corners might be best left to the professional, but a straightforward version can be made by anyone with moderate sewing skills.

Follow these few simple guidelines. Think about your cleaning options and choose your fabric carefully, as it will stand out. Use your eyes to fit the fabric to the frame. Where does the design fall? Do the motifs match and line up? The pattern is made using these steps: by measuring the frame, adding an extra half inch for seam allowance, laying out the pattern pieces on the fabric to factor in scale and repeat, and figuring out how the design will fall on the front so that it can be divided to create two door panels. The whole pattern comprises just six pieces: top, back, two sides, and two door panels. If you add a valance, you need to create an additional pattern. (Keep it under eight inches deep for easy access to the interior.) Measure everything twice before cutting, to avoid errors. To save on costs, use an inexpensive solid fabric for the closet's back panel, which will be hidden if it sits against a wall.

Velcro closures are perfect for the door panels, and easy to attach. We used Velcro tabs to close the doors down the center and two one-way dressmaker's zippers at the top to allow access to the interior. The door panels overlap one inch in each direction.

Use trims carefully; take your cues from the fabric. Grosgrain ribbon, up to two inches wide, works well, adding contrast and definition. Valances can add a note of fantasy not out of keeping with an unconventional piece like this—have fun with your design.

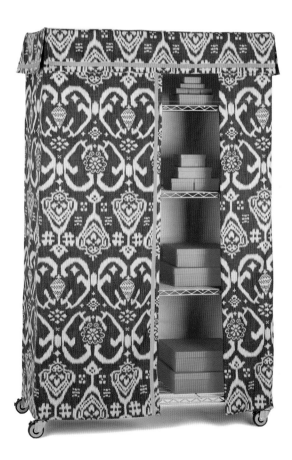

decorator's tips

- For mobility and looks, we wanted the wheels to be unencumbered. But for safety's sake, the wheels can also be locked.

- Use your eye to fit the fabric to the frame. Where does the design fall, and do the motifs match and line up? Remember: measure twice, cut once.

- Be creative, but don't go overboard. Use trims carefully; restraint keeps the unit chic.

- To save on costs, use an inexpensive solid fabric for the closet's back panel, which will be hidden if the panel sits against a wall.

- For easy access to the interior, keep valances no more than eight inches deep.

- Grosgrain ribbon trim adds contrast and definition. We used ribbon up to two inches wide.

Above: *Walls and bed meld into one with the application of a pastoral green-and-white Oriental-themed toile. Despite the narrative quality of the scene, it is not necessary that the pattern flow perfectly onto the headboard; this allows for the bed to be moved elsewhere in the room.*

Opposite: *A scene of insects in flight appears on a slipcovered headboard handsomely welted with solid black trim. The pattern repeats on the pillowcases. Other bed pillows match a fabric-covered chair, while a slipcovered circular footstool echoes a striped blanket.*

Opposite: *In a guest bedroom able to accom-modate two single beds, toile-covered headboards complement plaid bedspreads. An unexpected decorative element, hand-painted china plates and platters, link the room's colors and patterns. Simple white curtains and pillow-cases keep the low-ceilinged room bright.*

Above: *A double row of nailheads outlines the shape of the headboard, distinguished by notched corners, shapes that are subtly echoed in the drape of the curtains. The nail-heads add a masculine touch to the feminine fabric on the headboard.*

Above: Tea for two can be taken at a small table dressed with a sunny yellow plaid cloth laid over another cloth featuring an extravagant floral pattern. Chairs are covered with an oversized black-and-yellow gingham check.

Opposite: The hallmarks of a country-style room: exposed beams, a tile fireplace surround, bare wood floors, and ample sunshine. A blue tablecloth whose design features pastoral flora and fauna is the perfect unifying backdrop.

furniture construction:
good, better, best

good Usually made from wooden frames, which can be solid or composite, finger-jointed (which is less expensive), and most often made from a green wood like poplar or ash. Sometimes inexpensive frames are made from fiberboard (wood reconstituted from dust and ground scrap), which is not desirable. Joints are nailed or stapled together. This fastening usually lasts five to eight years, at which point the joints often loosen, since glue breaks down and nails or staples separate slowly over time through wear and tear. This is why upholsterers "reglue" a frame before reworking it.

The seat will contain zipper, or "z" springs in the seat. Inexpensive and less labor-intensive to install, these springs are adequate, but will eventually sag with use. In the back cushion, webbing rather than springs will be used, covered in polyfoam and Dacron. The seat will be covered in polyfoam with some foxedge, and the cushions are usually made from foam with Dacron wrap; some may also have cotton batting. Burlap fabric is often used under the finished fabric, rather than more costly muslin. Staples driven by a compressor are used to attach all materials to the wood frame.

In this category of sofa, pattern matching is often not completely uniform (if a patterned fabric rather than a solid color is used). There may be places where the pattern has been matched (usually the seat to the back), but other places where the pattern does not match (the arms, and skirt to the base), this being a cost-cutting measure on the manufacturer's part, as less fabric is wasted. Also, the seams in the self-welt are often not hidden—a minor but important detail. Costs in this category are usually $250–$400 per foot (for example, a seven-foot sofa would cost $1,750 to $2,800), including the manufacturer-supplied fabric. Customer's own material (fabric supplied by the consumer, abbreviated as COM) charges on a basic seven-foot sofa are approximately $2,000.

better Sofas in this category usually have frames made from kiln-dried, solid hardwoods like poplar, maple, or ash that might contain imperfections like knots or slightly crooked boards. The frame can be glued and nailed, but more often has a glue-and-dowel construction, or a combination of both. Joints that take a great deal of stress, such as those between seat deck and arms, are usually doweled. Depending on usage, these sofas are likely to last eight to ten years before re-gluing is needed. Springs can comprise a broad variety—combining several different ones provides dozens of possibilities for upholstery. These include "Marshall" units (prefabricated, tied coil springs, available in numerous sizes, which help to avoid the labor costs of hand-tied springs and provide the same structural support); and coil springs (the most popular), which are attached to the frame with manufactured clips and a network of jute webbing. Coil springs may be hand-tied up to eight ways in this price category ($400–$700 per foot), but a more usual number is four. The aforementioned zipper spring is the standard for seat backs, although Marshall units as well as rubberized webbing can also be used.

In ascending order of price, cushions are usually composed of a combination of polyfoam, cotton batting, bonded Dacron, down, feather blends, and (rather rarely) horsehair, so the combination used will affect the final cost of the upholstered piece. Burlap is usually used for internal support, and, depending on the manufacturer, a final muslin covering is sometimes attached under the finished upholstery. The reason for this is to be sure that the final form has the desired shape and contour, and that the "return" (the manner in which furniture returns to its original shape after someone has sat on it) is

Garlands of flowers wind their way across the embroidered linen cushions on this French daybed. Curtain valances are trimmed in pink and a rose-themed chintz was used for the curtains.

quick, and requires little adjustment by the consumer. Adjustments are often made here for the sake of the best final result. Again, staples from a compressor-driven gun are standard for attaching materials to the frame.

In this category, the pattern is most often engineered to match within the entire piece, sometimes with the exception of the outside back (since it often faces a wall, the construction of medium-quality upholstery may not concern itself with what is usually hidden from view). If you have chosen the fabric yourself (which is likely in this category), expect the upholsterer to require an "overage" in the fabric order to allow for the perfect match of the pattern. Upon completion, unused fabric is customarily returned to the client or decorator.

It is also typical for an upholsterer to add on a percentage, or "upcharge" for many details not usually so charged in the Good category, but included in the Best category because of the higher price point. For instance, you can expect to pay upcharges for trims of any kind (cord on seams, contrast welt, fringe or trims, nail heads, and dressmaker's details (such as waterfall skirts, bows, and other decorative flourishes). Standard upcharges directly relate to the labor/time equation the upholsterer employs to factor the final cost. If an additional six hours are required for the detail in question, the upholsterer will consider the cost per hour and add the percentage. Thus, a simple cord welt instead of fabric-covered welting might require a 10% upcharge, while a detailed and complicated nail-head finish, which requires one nail to be installed at a time, may incur as much as a 40% upcharge or more, depending on the degree of detail.

Upcharges should be discussed at the outset so that there are no surprises later. If a change is required after the price has been agreed upon, the upholsterer should provide a "change order" specifying the upcharge, and a signed or initialed copy should be returned to the upholsterer. In this way, the cost adjustment is firmly understood by all parties. This is standard procedure in regard to this type of work in this category.

The intermediate price range has the highest number of variables with regard to materials, structural support, construction methods, and details, and is of course the widest. It's also important to note here that the fabric (and any trims) are COM—and not included in the labor cost. Thus, the price quoted by the upholsterer rarely includes the finish fabric unless he or she is a supplier of upholstery materials, which can be purchased separately. One should expect to pay $400–$700 per foot without fabric.

This is probably the kind of sofa that most people purchasing a custom-made piece will buy. As such, pay extremely close attention to the shape, form, support, and longevity of style, as this sofa can be reupholstered again and again, approximately every five to ten years, for the rest of the owner's lifetime, and even into their children's lifetimes.

best Wooden frames of this type are exclusively made of hardwood, usually clear and of first quality. For interior pieces, maple, ash, walnut, or a combination of the latter may be used; woods suitable for exterior sofas can run the gamut from maple to mahogany to more exotic (and thus expensive) hardwoods. Note, however, that many exotic woods are disappearing from use as governments and regulators limit their harvesting and supply. Frames of this type often have exposed wood arms or legs made from the finest hardwoods. Excellent craftsmanship and elaborate hand carving, such as might be found on a ball-and-claw foot, add unique character to the frames, as well as aesthetic and monetary value.

This is a class of furniture in which additional woods are most frequently used. Legs may be made of tiger maple, or mahogany, and are attached to the structural frame with the same conservationist method used for the interior. Either doweled or dovetailed to the frame, the secondary woods add a luxurious touch to the piece. It may also be noted that while the front legs and exposed plinth of a sofa or chair may be an exotic, the back legs can often be made of a slightly less costly wood, although still one of good quality.

Construction techniques on these sofas include tongue and groove, dovetail joints, dowel and boring hole, and nails. All these techniques require the use of an excellent quality wood glue, which is necessary to maintain the jointures. Staples, nails or screws, and metal bracing are usually excluded in this category. Close attention to construction detailing, as well as adequate curing allowances, are standard.

With regard to the infrastructural materials used in the upholstery process, let's see what is used in less expensive furniture, and what replaces it in this higher quality category. Inexpensive burlap is often replaced with plain weave cottons, and polyfoam is rarely if ever used, but rather is replaced by a combination of wool batting, cotton batting, down and feather cushions or pads, and horsehair (either pure or blended with a mix of synthetic fiber or hoghair). Bonded Dacron is rarely selected, and is replaced by muslin or feather pads. Marshall units are replaced by meticulous eight-way hand-tied coil springs. Jute webbing (or rubberized webbing) on seat backs is supplanted by softer tensioned coil springs, and eight-way hand-tied coil springs. Perhaps the most important and cost-increasing detail in the fabrication of these sofas is the use of tacks rather than compressor-driven staples—applied one at a time in an extremely time-consuming process to attach all materials in the upholstered piece to the wooden frame.

One benchmark test for the quality of a well-made piece of furniture is its weight. Lifting a finished example of an upholsterer's work, as well as closely inspecting the finish details, can provide the consumer with a great deal of information. Because all the components of the "Best" quality piece weigh more by far (e.g., poplar vs. maple or coil springs vs. polyfoam), testing the weight of a piece (bend your knees!) will give one an idea of the price point. An upholstery firm's reputation is also very important in this class of furniture, since the price point is high. So asking for references is totally acceptable.

In this price range, one can expect nothing but perfection (within reason) from fabric placement. The only caveats here might be an unusual or difficult fabric, not normally used for upholstery; or a fabric that is awkward to place owing to its fiber content. The "Best" category upholsterer is likely to call a meeting to discuss such textiles and possible solutions. Assuming that the chosen finish fabric is an upholstery standard, meetings may be required to discern either the client or the decorator's wishes as to how the finish pattern will be placed. A cautious upholsterer will want to understand all the details and nuances of how a fabric may lay out, and ask pertinent questions where applicable. One example would be the choice of an embossed velvet: although the nap may change color when used in a particular fashion, the consumer may opt to accept this color variation in the interest of avoiding what they might consider to be unattractive seams on a tight-backed sofa. This decision could be resolved either way, but must be agreed upon before a $150-per-yard or better fabric has been cut incorrectly, leaving all parties at a loss to figure out whose responsibility it was to make such decisions. In the Best category, once all decisions have been made to satisfy the consumer and answer the upholsterer's questions, notes documenting all the decisions may be initialed by all parties to avoid misunderstandings later.

As one might assume, top-quality upholstery, with its long list of hand-worked detailing, comes with a hefty price tag: $800–$1,000 per foot. The upside is that the Best lasts longer, feels better, and looks better (upon close inspection) than anything else. In the Best category, the "upcharge" noted in the previous category is often dispensed with, as the price point is usually high enough to encompass any added flourishes.

about fabric

Brocade A heavy, luxurious fabric with raised designs that resemble embroidery, and accented with metallic threads. The figures in the intricate patterns of brocade are woven more loosely than those of damask. Instead of silk, manufacturers today string their looms with cotton warp yarns and use rayon and synthetic filling yarns. Despite their elegant design effects, true brocades are unsuitable for upholstery as the fabric snags and abrades easily, and is difficult, if not impossible to clean. Many fabrics now called brocades include simpler designs in tighter weaves that serve beautifully in upholstery applications.

Burlap A course, heavy fabric that used to be known as gunnysack, this utilitarian textile woven from jute or hemp fibers has found myriad uses, including wrapping, furniture manufacture, and of course, sacks. In upholstery, burlap bands provide the base for springs, and the fabric often surrounds necessary filling elements as in fox edges.

Canvas A heavy, tightly woven fabric made from cotton, linen, or hemp. Renowned for its strength and durability, the modern loom offers many weights of this indispensable textile. Its value came from its use as sails and tents, but the refinement of today's canvas allows furniture designers to employ this fabric on the outside of their creations as well as on the inside. Furniture upholstered in canvas encompasses all the advantages mentioned above, in addition to the fact that most dirt and stain are easily removed with a professional steam cleaning.

Chenille A tufted fabric in wool, cotton, or rayon, but cotton and cotton-synthetic blends are the most common. The tufts of pile appear in either in straight lines or in simple patterns. Unlike velvet, chenille is an informal fabric, and even with hard use, it revives nicely with a good washing or vacuuming. The more refined versions can be used for upholstery, and all versions make suitable slipcovers.

Chintz This cotton fabric originated in India, where flowered prints and a glossy texture made it ideal for everything from summer dresses to upholstery, depending on the weight of the fabric. The glossiness of the material was originally achieved by a satin weave, but today's textiles often imitate this effect with chemical treatments, in the same manner as most polished cottons. Chintz owes its most elaborate and celebrated designs to the British, who are often credited with its widespread use and popularity. Highly suitable for upholstery, a resin finish will withstand washing and dry cleaning.

Corduroy A durable cotton fabric recognized by a narrow, short pile along the straight grain (vertical), referred to as "cords" or "wale." The heaviness of the wale determines the weight of the cloth and its uses, as well as its nomenclature. The heavier the cloth, the wider the wale. Corduroy is especially popular in the manufacture of winter trousers and jackets, but just as the elbows and knees of these garments have been reinforced by tailors over the centuries, so will the arms and edges of furniture require reinforcement from wear with arm and back covers, or protected with the classic upholstery armor—the doily.

Cotton A fibrous material that forms soft, billowing clumps around the seeds of tropical plants of the mallow family. Unlike synthetic fibers, cotton "breathes" and absorbs liquid because the fibers are hollow. In nature, cotton fibers are curled, but the process called mercerization straightens them into long, straight rods, creating fibers that can be spun into strong, glossy threads and that easily accept dyes. The applications of this natural fiber are too numerous to list, and combined with other fibers, they make fabrics with the simultaneous advantages of beauty, durability, and easy care.

Crepe A fabric that can be woven in many different fibers and weights, crepe is distinguished by either a crinkled surface, or a slightly rough surface that resembles a dull moss. Wool crepe in the "mossy" weave imparts a classic, dignified appearance, wears very well, and is easily cleaned.

Crewel Refers to a type of embroidery using 2-ply wool yarn in different colors on a plain woven cotton or linen cloth. The motifs are usually flowers, vines, leaves, and small birds in a flowing design. Although the word crewel derives from an Old Welsh word meaning "wool," silk and linen were the preferred threads by the Middle Ages. Traditional crewel work features a great variety of stitches and rich colors, and trade with India influenced many of the English designs in the seventeenth century. Modern fabric mills produce a fabric of the same name that uses weaving techniques to imitate the look of embroidery.

Damask Named for the city of Damascus, the center of the fabric trade in the fourth century, damask was originally a silk fabric woven in China. Commonly woven today of cotton, rayon, or various blends, the fabric features traditional designs and motifs—often large flowers and stylized leaves—woven in a single color, or two. The designs stand out on the flat fabric because of the contrast of a slightly lustrous satin weave of the background with the matte sateen weave of the figures, which makes it reversible. Ideal for upholstery, cotton damask wears well, sheds dirt, and retains its original appearance after laundering.

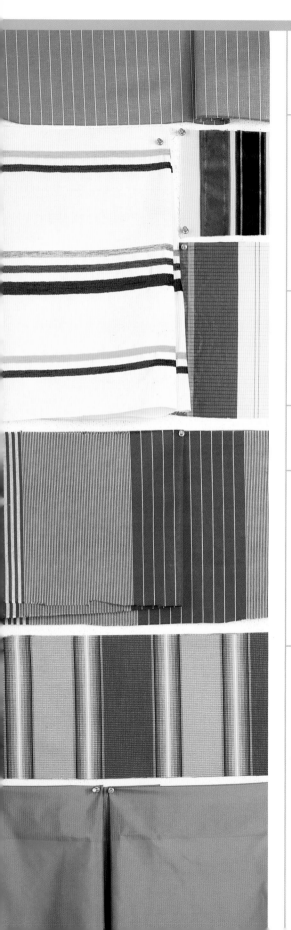

Denim A firm, hard-wearing cotton in a twill weave. Traditional denim is woven with blue warp threads and white filling threads. It offers the same qualities in furniture as it does in blue jeans—durability and easy care.

Dupioni silk The term derives from the Italian word for double, referring to the silk filament from cocoons that are either interlocked or are so cramped that they must be spun together. This produces a tough thread with small, irregular slubs. The silk is usually dyed in bright colors and may be woven with an iridescent, two-color sheen that is created with warp threads of one color and weft threads of another. Dupioni is a courser, tougher fabric than silk shantung, although both types may use fine, regular threads for the warp, and the slubbed threads for the waft, producing a subtle texture only in the horizontal direction.

Gingham A cotton or cotton-blend woven in plain weave with a checkered or striped pattern. In authentic gingham, yarn-dyed threads produce the checked effect on the loom rather than a fabric printing process. Gingham prints impart a homespun look, and its suitability for furniture depends on a fabric with enough body, and an informal room.

Ikat Can refer to the technique of tie-dying yarn before it is woven into cloth, or to the fabric that is produced by this method.

Jacquard The complex weaving process is named for its founder, Joseph Marie Jacquard, who invented it between 1801 and 1804. The Jacquard loom makes possible the most intricate patterns and designs by means of a series of punched cards, controlled by a mechanism above the loom. Each card determines the position the warp threads for a single woven row, that is, the passage of the shuttle one time across the loom. Every pattern requires a unique set of punched cards. Damasks, brocades, tapestries and many other fabrics are woven on Jacquard looms. Today, computer technology has replaced the punched cards.

Jute A glossy, rough fiber from either of two East Indian plants of the linden family, woven into burlap fabric or twisted into twine.

Linen The oldest known fabric made from the fibers of the flax plant, linen is usually loomed in a plain weave. Strength, coolness, crispness, and a natural luster are its trademarks, but the fabric wrinkles very easily. Combining linen with other fibers greatly lessens wrinkling.

Matelassé Another wonderful product of the Jacquard loom, the word matellassé is derived from the French term meaning "quilted." Two sets of warp and weft threads combine in intricate combinations to form a slightly raised patterns, most often in a single color. These subtle designs resemble quilting and are found in many decorator fabrics and in very expensive linens.

Muslin A plain woven cotton fabric that can be light to very heavy.

Polyester A synthetic fiber made from long chains—a polymer—of an ester molecule. Noted for crease resistance, color retention, strength, and durability, polyester can be spun with other fibers or woven with natural yarns to impart these qualities in myriad types of textiles. Unlike the natural yarns of wool, linen, and cotton, polyester is not absorbent or breathable.

Rayon The regenerated cellulose of wood pulp and other vegetable matter is extruded through tiny holes to produce the smooth textile fiber known as rayon. The smoothness of the fiber creates fabrics that drape exceptionally well, but fabric mills usually combine rayon with other fibers for durability.

Sailcloth A heavy cotton canvas.

Sateen A cotton yarn in a satin weave, sateen is smooth with a soft hand. Its durability and low luster make it an excellent all-around decorator fabric.

Satin Usually made of rayon, cotton, or silk, satin is a type of weave where the warp threads lay over several weft threads in succession before a weft thread takes them to the back of the cloth. While the face of satin fabrics is smooth and shiny, the reverse is dull, and slightly rough. The weaving technique that produces the beautiful sheen also makes very shiny satin fabrics susceptible to pulled threads and abrasion.

Silk A fabric woven from the fine, continuous fiber produced by the silk-worm for its cocoon. Despite their very light weight, silk threads possess very high tensile strength and medium elasticity. Unless combined with other fibers, such as wool, upholstery applications for this fiber are limited by its tendency to abrade and difficulty to clean.

Moisture, robust wear, and ultraviolet light are the three enemies of silk. If it seems likely that any of these harmful elements will be present, it is probably best to choose another type of fabric, or one of the many beautiful faux silks available in today's market. These man-made fibers mimic the physical appearance of silk but eliminate the dilemmas presented by its physical limitations.

Taffeta Said to have originated in Persia, (taftah—a fine silk fabric), a fine cross rib imparts crispness to this plain weave fabric with a medium sheen and smooth on both sides. Generally woven in rayon, synthetics, or silk, and available in many prints and weights, taffeta is primarily used in formal wear.

Tapestry A heavy, handwoven fabric in which intricate pictorial designs or scenes are woven or applied on a ground fabric. In machine-made tapestry, the complex pictures are achieved using several filling threads with a single warp. Unlike hand-woven tapestry, the machine-made type is not reversible.

Ticking A strong cotton, tightly woven with more warp threads than filling threads. The tight plain weave makes the fabric feather-proof, hence its use as a covering for mattresses and pillows. Traditionally offered in yarn-dyed stripes, but flowered prints and simple designs are also available.

Toile A plain-woven cotton fabric printed with monochromatic vignettes of rural life, historical events, pastoral, genre, and mythological scenes.

Velvet Velvet, a fabric woven by the simplest of methods, consists of a warp and a filler, which are woven together much like a hook rug, with raised loops. After the weaving process, the fabric is cut to remove the connecting ends of the loops, leaving a velour finish. Velvets are woven of synthetic fibers, cotton, linen, and silk, as well as blends. All velvets, however, have a directional orientation: the fabric is compacted by the cutting process toward one direction, and this produces variations in tone when viewed from different angles. Careful attention must be paid to mark the direction in which the fabric will be used. This is usually done with safety pins or tailor's chalk on the reverse of the cut. Failing this, the finished product might appear to be of several different shades.

A second reason for careful consideration when working with velvet is the "nap" produced by the loop-cutting process. Velvet has directional quality not only with regard to color, but in reference to the "hand" or "tooth" as well. Running your hand up a cut of velvet the "wrong" way meets with resistance and crushes the nap, causing the fabric to apparently change color. While running your hand down a cut of velvet, the fabric feels soft and subtle; the velvet may mark from the hand movement, but soft brushing with a natural fiber brush will remove the mark.

As with silk, velvet does not wear well under certain conditions—most notably moisture and crushing. A short, dense pile is common to all velvets, be they cotton, silk, or rayon. The soft pile, beautiful luster, and exquisite drape have made velvet irresistible for centuries. Cotton velvet makes a good choice in upholstery for its relative durability, heavier weight, and subtle luster. Although velvet is unsuitable for furniture that sees heavy use, professional cleaning delivers good results.

Viscose A type of rayon that undergoes a treatment with chemicals and a special spinning process. Many fine decorator fabrics contain viscose rayon yarns for their durability and luster.

Wool fabric made from the fibers of animal coats, usually sheep, that can be spun and woven in innumerable combinations. Few materials retain their beauty like wool, or breath, wear, and clean as well as this natural fiber.

glossary

Bias cut When a fabric is cut from one from one corner to its opposite, diagonal corner. When fabric is "cut on the bias," the weave in the direction of the slant with be elastic.

Box pleat Two pleats folded to the back of the fabric in opposite directions so that the outside fold of each pleat meets in the center, creating a box. When the pleats are folded to the front of the fabric, the box pleat is called a kick pleat.

Button tufting Tufting is actually a form of quilting—very much like tied quilts. Cords that are drawn through the upholstery and tied to the back of the frame secure the upholstery filling in place. As the cords create "puffs and valleys" when they are pulled to the back of the frame, they are positioned to form patterns like diamonds or squares. Fabric-covered buttons accentuate the pattern and cover the small holes where each cord has been drawn through the fabric.

Camelback A sofa with a curved back or with a hump in the center.

Colorfast All fabrics are rated for their level of color retention. Fabrics classified as colorfast are those that under normal conditions will not suffer noticeable fading or other loss of color from cleaning or sunlight during the life of the fabric. A sofa receiving direct sunlight all day in front of a picture window would not be considered a normal condition.

Colorway A term used in design to describe a certain color combination.

Deck The flat platform underneath the cushion of an upholstered chair or sofa. In fine furniture, the deck of a chair or sofa will be upholstered in the same fabric as the rest of the chair. In this way, as the cushions change shape with age allowing the edges of the deck to be visible, the deck will match the rest of the piece.

Double ending A technique that is used to match geometric prints, such as plaids by marking and sewing a center point, them stitching slowly and carefully from each end toward the center.

Dowel A wooden cylinder that fits into a matching hole to hold two pieces of wood together, then glued. Fine furniture often features dowelled joints, the necessary method of jointure before the mass production of nails and screws.

Dressmaker details The type of detailing one finds on fine clothing, such as bows made in contrasting fabrics, designs in passementerie, pleats made in lining fabric, etc.

Filling threads *See* Weft.

Finger-joint A technique used to combine short pieces of wood into a longer piece. The pieces are fitted together by shaping one end of a board into wedges that are fitted into the end of another board, with opposite shaping—resembling interlocking fingers. After applying adhesive, the interlocking edges form a strong, durable joint. Finger joints can also be made with crenellated edges.

Flange An edge of cloth that is used as an anchor or support. *See* Welting and Fox roll.

Flocking Tiny bits of cotton or wool fibers called flock are applied to a ground fabric with adhesive to form patterns. Some flocked fabrics imitate the look of cut velvet.

Fox edge This time-saver for upholsterers is also known as "edge roll." It consists of a long roll made of burlap, canvas, or some other utilitarian fabric that is stuffed with polyester or batting and has a wide edge or flange of fabric running along one side. Mounted around the rim of coil seats or the arms of chairs, it creates smooth, rounded edges.

Gauffrage A process of imparting the special effects of crimping, plaiting and fluting to fabric by means of a hot iron or other heat process.

Gimp A tightly woven trim resembling a fancy braid. It can be used to decorate everything from curtains to lampshades, but is especially useful to cover upholstery edges where the fabric meets the wood on a piece of furniture. Today, it is a simple matter to find gimp to match any complex jacquard or brocade, as manufacturers offer the trim in innumerable color combinations as well as solids. Gimp was used almost exclusively before the advent of double welting.

Grosgrain ribbon A mainstay of the dressmaking and millinery trades, this substantial ribbon can be quickly identified by its horizontal cords. Usually manufactured of rayon or polyester, grosgrain ribbon wears well and can be washed in water. It is available in a seemingly infinite array of colors and widths.

Ground This term refers to the background color on which another pattern prints. In large, busy prints, the ground can be nearly invisible.

Interlining In furniture, an interlining is a lining that is sewn between the outside upholstery fabric and the inside fabric to give stability to lighter or "slippery" fabrics, and to improve wear. They can be sewn into curtains as well to give opacity and body and to protect face fabrics from sunlight.

Knit backing In a process developed to give body and manageability to lightweight or fragile fabrics, a thin knitted textile is fused to the wrong side of the fabric. Fine brocades, chenille, lightweight velvets and all silks are excellent candidates for this treatment, and while knit backing not only increases the life of the fabric, it also prevents seams from falling apart prematurely. Alson known as "fabric backing."

Marshall units Also known as "spring units," this type of support was named for the man who developed them for the manufacture of mattresses. A unit consists of a pre-compressed spring coil that is covered in two or three layers of cotton, which are known as "pockets." Linked together with hog rings, Marshall units can be combined to any shape or size seat.

Miter Literally, to join two perpendicular pieces at an angle. A mitered hem is one in which the fabric on a corner is turned under, folded, and stitched evenly at a 45-degree angle, unlike a square hem, where one side simply overlaps the other. Mitering creates neater and less bulky corners.

Passementerie A very narrow braid or cord (traditionally black) that is sewn onto a garment in complex, intertwined patterns. In prior centuries, new patterns for these designs were in great demand.

Pattern matching This term refers to the work of laying out a design in such a way that the pattern of stripes, checks, plaids, etc. continues unbroken across the seams. When this technique is well done, the seams will be nearly invisible, as they disappear into the fabric pattern.

Pattern repeat We speak of a pattern repeat when referring to one complete motif or design unit that is duplicated down the length of the fabric. Knowing the length and width of the pattern repeat is necessary to accurately calculate the amount of fabric needed when matching patterns across seams or centering the design on upholstery pieces.

Railroading As in tailoring, upholstery and decorator patterns are usually cut on the straight grain of the fabric, or vertically. Railroading refers to the technique of cutting a pattern on the cross grain, or horizontally, to avoid numerous seams in large pieces, such as a dust ruffle on a bed, or the back of a large sofa.

Self-welting Describes welting that is made with the same fabric as the rest of the upholstery.

Selvage The narrow left and right borders of a length of cloth are called selvages. The weave of the selvages is heavier than the rest of the fabric for stability and to prevent raveling.

Single welting This type of welting is a single fabric-covered cord that lays atop an upholstered edge.

Warp The threads that run vertically from one end of a bolt of fabric to the other. A loom is strung with warp threads, and woven with weft threads.

Waterfalling The usual way upholstery fabric is laid on furniture, with the pattern running vertically. This method is also referred to as laying the pattern "up the roll."

Weft The threads on a loom that are woven horizontally between the warp threads. The weft is also referred to as "filling."

Welting A fabric-covered cord that is sewn into the upholstery seam to accent the shape of the piece and to strengthen the seam is called welting. The fabric left hanging on the edge of the covered cord is used to sew the welting into the seam and is referred to as the flange of the welting.

photography credits

Page 2: Tria Giovan
Pages 4–5: Tria Giovan
Page 8: Edmund Barr
Page 10: Thibault Jeanson
Page 12: Courtesy of *House Beautiful*
Page 14: Jonn Coolidge
Pages 16–63: Joshua Sheldon
Page 64: Simon Upton
Pages 64–65: Jeff McNamara
Page 66: Edmund Barr
Page 67: Minh + Wass
Page 68: Tim Street-Porter
Page 69: Jonn Coolidge
Page 70 (top): Tim Street-Porter
Page 70 (bottom): Jeff McNamara
Page 71: Courtesy of *House Beautiful*
Page 72: Courtesy of *House Beautiful*
Page 73: Jonn Coolidge
Page 74: Thibault Jeanson
Page 75: Courtesy of *Victoria* Magazine
Page 76: Simon Upton
Page 77: David Montgomery
Page 78: Sang An
Pages 80–102: Joshua Sheldon
Page 103: Courtesy of *House Beautiful*
Page 104: Courtesy of *House Beautiful*
Page 105: Elizabeth Zeschin
Page 106: Dana Gallagher
Page 107: Anthony Cotsifas
Page 108: Gabi Zimmerman
Page 109: Courtesy of *House Beautiful*
Page 110: David Montgomery
Page 111: Jonn Coolidge
Page 112 (top): Oberto Gili
Page 112 (bottom): Peter Margonelli

Page 113: Courtesy of *House Beautiful*
Page 114: Tom McWilliam
Page 115: Carlos Emilio
Page 116 (top): Simon Upton
Page 116 (bottom): Fernando Bengoechea
Page 117: Courtesy of *House Beautiful*
Page 118: Susan Gentry McWhinney
Page 119: Dominique Vorillon
Page 120: David Prince
Page 121: Dana Gallagher
Page 122: Thibault Jeanson
Pages 124–138: Joshua Sheldon
Page 139: Minh + Wass
Pages 140–141: Jeff McNamara
Page 142: Gordon Beall
Page 143: Scott Frances
Page 144: Alec Hemer
Pages 148–161: Joshua Sheldon
Page 162: William Waldron
Page 163: Victoria Pearson
Page 164 (top): Tria Giovan
Page 164 (bottom): Gabi Zimmerman
Page 165: Alec Hemer
Page 166: Eric Boman
Page 167: Carlos Emilio
Page 168: Alec Hemer
Pages 170–185: Joshua Sheldon
Page 186: Gabi Zimmerman
Page 187: Dominique Vorillon
Page 188: William Waldron
Page 189: Fernando Bengoechea
Page 190: Courtesy of *House Beautiful*
Page 191: Jeff McNamara
Page 193: Fernando Bengoechea

index